SARAH THE PRIESTESS

Alabaster head, from Ur. This sculpture of an
unknown woman evokes the image of Sarah,
with her visionary eyes . . . and silenced mouth.
University Museum, University of Pennsyvania.

SARAH THE PRIESTESS

The First Matriarch
of Genesis

SAVINA J. TEUBAL

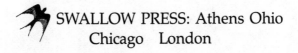 SWALLOW PRESS: Athens Ohio
Chicago   London

Second printing 1986.

Swallow Press books
are published by
Ohio University Press
Athens Ohio 45701

Maps drawn by Don McPeak
Book design by Hal Stevens

   Cover photograph En-anna-tumma, *en* priestess (statue dedicated to the Goddess Ningal). *University Museum, University of Pennsylvania.*

Cataloguing in Publication Data

Teubal, Savina J., 1926-
   Sarah the priestess.

   Bibliography: p.
   Includes index.
   1. Sarah (Biblical character) 2. Bible. O.T. Genesis — Criticism,
interpretation, etc. 3. Women and religion — Near East. I. Title.
BS580.S25T47   1984   222'.110924   84-96
ISBN 0-8040-0843-4
ISBN 0-8043-0844-2 (pbk.)

TO TANIA AND MARIA

CONTENTS

ILLUSTRATIONS

FOREWORD

Savina Teubal has undertaken a difficult task in writing her study *Sarah the Priestess.*

The only source in which Sarah is mentioned is the Book of Genesis, which contains a very few highly selective and rather enigmatic stories dealing with her. On the surface these stories tell very little about Sarah, and what they do tell is complicated and confused by the probability that it represents residue surviving from two different written sources based on two independent oral traditions. We are told that Sarah was the paternal half-sister of Abraham, her husband; that she was childless and gave her handmaid Hagar to be Abraham's concubine so that the child Hagar would bear would be considered Sarah's own, but some thirteen years later, at an age at which procreation had to be considered miraculous, Sarah did conceive and bear a son, Isaac; that she instructed Abraham to expel Hagar and her son Ishmael; that her beauty had attracted the attention of both Pharoah and Abimelech, the king of Gerar; and that she died at the age of 127 years and was buried in the Cave of Machpelah. It is, in the main, on this meager and fragmentary material that Dr. Teubal had to build her reconstruction of Sarah's position as a priestess, as a carrier of an old Mesopotamian religio-cultural tradition, and as a representative of a cult in which female functionaries played the main role.

How does she go about it? For one thing, she utilized data from ancient Mesopotamian (Sumerian, Babylonian) inscriptions which have a bearing on the role of women as priestesses in the religions of those lands during the thousand or so years preceding the period to which Abraham and Sarah are usually assigned. Then, in the light of what she could glean from these sources, she subjects every word contained in Genesis about Sarah — and about her successors in Abraham's family, namely Rebekah, Rachel, and Leah — to the most painstaking scrutiny. She pays special attention to every indication found in the Bible of a matriarchal or, as she most cautiously expresses herself, non-patriarchal social order.

Dr. Teubal's conclusions are, to say the least, surprising. Sarah emerges as a veritable matriarch, the heir of an old female priestly tradition to which she clings with determination even after her husband takes her to the Land of Canaan, with its patriarchal social tradition and order. Dr. Teubal shows that the "Sarah tradition" represents a non-patriarchal system struggling for survival in isolation, in the patriarchal environment of what was for Sarah a foreign society. She indicates that the insistence of Sarah and, of Rebekah that their sons and heirs marry wives from the old homeland had to do, not so much with preference for endogamy and cousin marriage, as with the intention of matriarchal priestesses to ensure the continuation of their old *kahina*-tradition against the overwhelming odds represented by patriarchal Canaan.

Has Dr. Teubal succeeded in presenting her thesis convincingly? This question cannot easily be answered. Some critics will argue that, for all her erudition and skillful marshalling of evidence, the case remains circumstantial. The fact cannot be changed that nowhere in Genesis, or in all Jewish tradition for that matter, is there a clear statement as to Sarah's priesthood. As Dr. Teubal states at the end of her conclusion, the very word *kohenet*, the female form of *kohan*, "priest," has not survived in the Biblical Hebrew vocabulary.

On the other hand, her theory sheds new light on the puzzling, highly energetic role Sarah and the other matriarchs play in the Genesis narratives — a role so active that it repeatedly overshadows that of their husbands. In a patriarchal environment such as that of the Canaan of Genesis, this role seems discordant and problematic. The difficulty, however, is eliminated if we understand, as Dr. Teubal suggests, that Sarah and the other matriarchs acted within a traditional Mesopotamian role-pattern of priestesses, of a class of women who retained a highly privileged position vis-à-vis their husbands, and who played a more decisive role than their husbands in directing the lives of their children. In addition to this major issue there are many other puzzling details in the Genesis narratives on which Dr. Teubal's investigations shed fresh light.

All in all, this study is a valuable piece of original research, which makes a considerable contribution to our understanding of the obscure origins of the role women play in the Genesis narratives.

RAPHAEL PATAI

PREFACE

My ideal, when I was young, was Abraham. I had visions of myself walking through the dusty land, talking with God as he had done. It never occurred to me that I should have looked for a heroine, not a hero. It never occurred to me that I should have chosen to emulate Sarah, not Abraham.

Why? Who were the women in Genesis, and in what way are they significant to us?

Many generations have delved into the biblical records in an effort to understand what men have achieved in the historical past, who men are and what they can become. It is against this historical perspective that men can measure themselves and their dreams in the present and in so doing validate their aspirations and achievements.

No such perspective is granted to women. Women are denied the ancient pillars of wisdom on which to structure their own aspirations and future achievements. This is not, so to speak, for want of ancient pillars. The pillars are there, waiting to be unearthed from the dust of patriarchal centuries.

For millenia, Western society has been based on codes of behavior affirmed or implied in our sacred scriptures. The stated codes, fairly straightforward, can be found in the books of Leviticus and Deuteronomy. "You shall not copy the practice of the land of Canaan to which I am taking you; nor shall you follow their customs," is an example from Leviticus; Deuteronomy states, "Cursed be he who lies with his sister, whether the daughter of his father or mother."

The implied codes, on the other hand, are more difficult to deal with because their meaning depends on interpretation. Abraham, for instance, received a command to sacrifice his son, and without hesitation he attempted to do so. Abraham's blind faith in and obedience to the command of his God, however extreme it might be, became an example to be followed by those who held the scriptures to be sacred. To them the story implies that we should all obey the word of God without question.

The Bible is the word of God. As I reread the Genesis narratives with a newly open mind, setting aside accepted interpretation and attending only to what is actually there, I realized that it is the interpretations of the commentators, not the texts themselves, which place the stories in patriarchal focus. I suggest that some of these narratives were originally tales from an oral tradition about women, and that these stories were later adapted and then modified to suit an evolving patriarchal situation clearly described in the narratives themselves.

Although my concern here is with women, it is not my intent to minimize the role of the patriarchs. Untold volumes have been written about them; but I have found in those volumes hardly any mention of the women, and what little there is, is often derisive. The patriarchs were essential in the establishment of a patriarchal system in their community. This was, however, against the better judgment of their wives. The struggle of the matriarchs against this cultural intrusion is impressively described in these stories, as we shall see.

A study of the ancients reveals that they were not as unsophisticated as we have been led to believe. In particular, women have traditionally been depicted as primitive and childish in their aspirations and generally lacking in vision. Fresh study of our female forebears, however, invalidates this view and shows us that the matriarchs were learned, wise women who were highly developed spiritually.

In my opinion, no group has been more maligned in the story of human progress than women. Our history books and religious texts are filled with the aspirations and dreams of men, rarely of women. But women too have entertained hopes and visions of a better world, although these have been distorted or frustrated by those of men.

The matriarchs of Genesis, seen in this new light, provide a positive image for Western women. Like young men, young women need a model to emulate, an ideal to strive for. The narratives show that respected, mature women, with spiritual influence and worldly position, are part of biblical history. It is only a matter of interpretation whether these women are seen in a negative or positive light. It is my hope that this study will contribute a positive light to the image of the ancient matriarchs.

ACKNOWLEDGEMENTS

It took me over seven years to research and write this book. It is especially meaningful to me that family and friends never failed in their interest and encouragement during that time.

In particular, I think of María Meredith Rutter, *hija de mi alma*, of her spirit of curiosity, her love and her interest, despite her tender years when the process of developing "Sarah" began.

Raphael Patai, mentor and friend, deserves my deepest gratitude for his guidance, his erudite comments, and his unfailing interest in the program of my work and its final publication.

Itala T. Rutter has helped me enormously over the years with her literary criticism, but most of all with her enthusiasm for, and faith in, the work itself, especially during the many periods in which I felt discouraged. To her, my very special heartfelt thanks.

In the early stages of my work I received invaluable suggestions and comments in their areas of expertise from Edith Benkov, Vern Carroll, David Noel Freedman, Tikva Simone Frymer, Rivkah Harris, John Huehnergard, Piotr Michalowsky, Michael O'Conner, Holly Prado and Adrienne Rich. I deeply appreciate the generosity with which they gave of their time and effort.

I cannot find words enough to thank my dear friend Alice Bloch for her wisdom and patience and time, reading and re-reading the last draft and final revision, with her profoundly Jewish insight.

I must pay special tribute to Phyllis Sherman of Swallow Press for her painstaking final revision. Her perceptive queries and intelligent suggestions helped me to successfully complete this lengthy project.

I am especially grateful to Velma Harlow for her friendship, intelligence and diligence in typing the manuscript.

A manuscript comes of age on publication, in the sense that it leaves the shelter of its author to stand on its own in the world. This transition depends entirely on the vision and expertise of a publisher. I am truly grateful to Morton Weisman of Swallow Press for his faith in my work and Patricia Elisar of Ohio University for her support.

INTRODUCTION

According to tradition, the Jewish Bible is made up of twenty-four books, the first five of which are referred to as Torah, Pentateuch, or "The Five Books of Moses." The first book is known by its Greek name, Genesis, or by its Hebrew name, Bereshith, which roughly mean "beginning," or "coming into being."

In the first eleven of its fifty chapters, the book of Genesis recounts the creation of the world and history of humanity, from the creation of Adam and Eve to the birth of the patriarch Abraham. The remaining chapters narrate the lives of four generations of descendants of the family of Terah:

1. Abraham and Sarah
2. Isaac and Rebekah
3. Jacob and Leah and Rachel
4. The Twelve Tribes of Israel

The protagonists of the Genesis narratives have always been understood to be Early Hebrews who left Mesopotamia, their homeland, with a new religion and culture that they brought to Canaan as the foundation of a new cultus. The narratives relate the stories of females and males equally, from the initial migration into Canaan, that of Sarah and Abraham, to the subsequent one, two generations later, by Rachel, Leah, and Jacob.

Wouldn't the new immigrants into Canaan have brought with them some part of the faith of their Mesopotamian background?

As I studied the history and literature of the ancient Near East of the period between the 25th and 15th centuries B.C.E. (Before the Common Era), and then reread the biblical material to try to fit it into a historical or literary perspective, I looked for religious elements in the Genesis stories that did not conform to Jewish thought or tradition.

In the story of Abraham the narratives begin with an account concerning Sarah and Pharoah and continue with this woman's trials in securing progeny. Finally, a whole chapter is dedicated to her place of burial. Of the forty-eight years of Abraham's life after Sarah's death there is no detail whatever. In other words, it is Sarah's role that furthers the story. Abraham is presented primarily as the strong warrior-consort who guards her rights and those of her offspring. That his progeny (Ishmael) by a concubine (Hagar) is also graced by the celestial authorities indicates that Abraham was worthy of his exceptional wife (Sarah), and therefore all his descendants were of princely stock.

If the narration of events following the death and burial of Sarah were truly patriarchal, it would deal with the life and exploits of the male heir, Isaac. Instead, once again the accent is on the role of a woman: Rebekah. About Isaac, her husband, we are told little relating to the establishment of the religious faith. He is a placid, sedentary man whose life is colored and influenced by the presence of his outstanding wife. Apart from the incident of the Akedah (The Binding of Isaac in which Abraham is commanded to sacrifice his son), we know nothing of the boyhood or youth of the supposed hero. "His" story begins with a detailed account of Rebekah's betrothal. Rebekah's story, like that of Sarah before her, records the trials before and after the birth of her sons. It is Rebekah who influences and directs Jacob, the son of her choice, who later becomes Israel, leader of the Hebrew Patriarchy proper.

My interest in the women deepened when I recognized that Sarah's actions in banishing Hagar and Ishmael need not be seen as those of a spiteful, jealous woman but could be explained on the basis of Mesopotamian law codes and, in certain instances, on regulations that applied only to women in the ranks of religious orders. It became clear to me that the issues between Sarah, Rebekah, and Rachel and their menfolk, as related in the Genesis narratives, are not individual personal disagreements but the result of the women's struggle to maintain certain principles over a period of three generations.

In the following investigations I give evidence to show that Sarah was a "priestess" whose intimate relationship with the supernatural made her privy to the mysteries of religions and endowed her with the power of the office that went with it. I also suggest that the particular office held by Sarah was the most elevated in rank and status, the most sacred and most revered — a position comparable to that of women known as *en* and *naditu* who belonged to religious orders in the ancient Mesopotamian region of Sumer.

In ancient times the moon represented the power of creativity and most frequently was personified by a Goddess. Social change that made property personal rather than communal brought the rise of male power and the patriarchal society, symbolized by the sun and the God. Sun worship and male priests superseded the earlier moon cults presided over by priestesses, though remnants of these remained at such shrines as Delphi and Paphos.

One function of ancient religious office was oracle-giving. Priestesses at this time acted as oracular prophets, providing military and political advice to rulers, and thus had a powerful if indirect influence on the affairs of state. It was the priestess, too — versed in astronomy — who advised the community of seasonal changes and astronomical conjunctions that affected the cycle of agriculture, and who prescribed the appropriate rituals for each occasion.

I have chosen as a model for Sarah the *en* and *naditu* women for two reasons: (1) the most extensive information on these particular "priestesses" comes from cuneiform tablets discovered in Mesopotamia; and (2) the *naditu* were associated both with Ur, the southern Sumerian city where Sarah's family originated, and Haran, the northern Mesopotamian city to which they moved. I would like to stress, however, that my use as a model of a priestess role of the period 3000–1500 B.C.E. does not mean that the Genesis stories concerned with women could not have originated in a different ethnic milieu before recorded times; they probably did.

In our extant biblical text, tales of female and male protagonists have been woven into a homogeneous pattern, revealing quite precisely customs and traditions of Mesopotamia and Canaan known to us from their laws and literature. While the tales may reflect actual migrations in some instances, in others they may be ancient stories of traditional folklore that were later applied to historic situations. For example, the story of Sarah's emigration from Mesopotamia to Canaan may well represent the migration from Haran to Hebron of a group or tribe led by a priestess. But the personal story of Sarah and Hagar, which follows in detail the codes of Hammurapi and Lipit Ishtar, could have been part of a legend of actual heroines who may or may not have been Hebrew matriarchs.

No reason is given in the texts for the choice of Canaan over Mesopotamia as the setting for the development of a new faith. Abraham is told "Go forth from your native land and from your father's house to a land that I will show you," with the promise that he will acquire a great name and blessings and will father a great nation. No mention is made of founding a new religion. Abraham took Sarah, his priestess wife, with him. As will become evident in the following chapters, it was Abraham who was influenced by the social and religious customs of Canaan against the better judgment of Sarah. Had Sarah and her matriarch successors not been isolated in a foreign land, they would have commanded more authority over their husbands, who instead absorbed the patriarchal values of the Canaanites.

In the chapters that follow, the name Abram will be used for the patriarch rather than Abraham because the latter name conjures up a wealth of characteristics with which the patriarch has been endowed. In using the lesser known version of the patriarch's name, I think it will be easier for the reader to visualize Sarah's husband, Abram, without preconceived ideas.

Likewise ye wives, be in subjection to your own husbands . . .
Even as Sarah obeyed Abraham, calling him lord. . . .

1 Peter 3:1,6

SARAH THE PRIESTESS

PART ONE
SOCIAL IMPLICATIONS

"Whatever Sarah Tells You, Do as She Says" (Gen. 21:12)

Because the Genesis narratives have been interpreted and commented on by scholars almost exclusively from a patriarchal point of view, they are often confusing, contradictory, or simply difficult to follow.[1] But some of these passages can be understood, despite their often enigmatic nature, if they are taken as depicting a society that was not strictly patriarchal. On closer examination of the texts, it appears that the women of the stories were struggling to maintain traditions and customs not always in accord with those of their husbands or fathers; and this struggle, though discernible in the text, is not directly acknowledged.

Within the framework of the Old Testament, these stories are a bridge between pre-history and history, between legend and fact. I suggest that the conflict in the narratives represents the tremendous changes occurring between the pre-historical and historical periods, with the matriarchs symbolizing the pre-history of the Hebrews, and the patriarchs, the beginnings of Israelite history.

In the broadest sense, the Old Testament is composed of tales that fall into three successive categories: first, stories of individuals; second, of families; and last, of tribes or nations. Except for the creation and downfall of Eve, all the stories in the first category are about men. The third category is similar to the first in that respect. In the occasional record of the courage or enterprise of a woman, such as Esther, Ruth, or Huldah, the women are described as supporting the interests and activities of men. But in the second category, which begins with the account of the migration of Terah and his descendants from Mesopotamia to Canaan, we find that the focus of the narratives is overwhelmingly on women and their aspirations. It is precisely in this portion of Genesis, that which deals with the family, that we find episodes difficult to understand.

3

For example, incest is outlawed in most societies today and was in antiquity. But is it permitted in Genesis? Sarah is married to her brother. It is puzzling also that we are given more information on the background of Sarah's niece Milcah than on Sarah, the ancestress of Israel. And why did Abram and Isaac prefer to say to kings that they were the brothers rather than the husbands of their wives, permitting their wives to be taken? Why did Rachel remove the teraphim, the sacred images, when she left her father's house? Why Rachel and not Leah, the eldest? These episodes, and many others in the Genesis texts, are bewildering only if they are seen as occurring in a patriarchal society.

H. M. Orlinsky, in defining what he describes as "a relatively simple [patriarchal] social structure" in Genesis, maintains: "The father was the head of the family. The sons and daughters, with the spouses and children, were all subject to the authority of the patriarch. By tribal law, the oldest son succeeded the father upon his death." A few pages later: "In actual life, however, the matriarch too was a dominant figure, for example Abraham's wife Sarah and Isaac's wife Rebekah." That is, "In the domestic sphere, the woman's ameliorative counsels and her motherly feelings were taken seriously."[2]

But ameliorative counsel and motherly feelings are devoid of social authority, particularly when they are expressed only in the domestic sphere. The vivid stories depicting Sarah's removal of Ishmael from the line of inheritance, Rebekah's triumph over Esau, and Rachel's appropriation of the teraphim despite Laban's agitated effort to retrieve them clearly show the effort by fathers and husbands to gain control of a non-patriarchal system existing at the time. And the matriarchs are depicted as well aware of their diminishing rights as kinswomen. The picture of the women as headstrong and emotional reveals a later explanatory gloss by redactors forced to deal with strongly non-patriarchal traditions.

In these so-called patriarchal narratives, descent is actually traced through the mother. But matrilineal descent is not taken into account by scholars attempting to justify the marriage of Sarah and Abram. Again, evidence of succession by the youngest (ultimogeniture) can be found in Genesis, not only in the narratives but also in the genealogies. The famous lists of "begettings" were attempts made by priestly scribes to change the pattern and trace the descent of the Hebrews exclusively through the male line.

These "patriarchal" narratives are filled with episodes in which the will of the matriarchs overrides that of their husbands because in certain areas they command superior authority — authority that in some cases is clearly upheld by the deity. This is movingly witnessed by Abram, who must accept the banishment of his son Ishmael from Hebron, where Sarah lives. "Whatever Sarah tells you, do as she says," his God tells him. Unable to oppose Sarah's command, Abram follows Hagar and Ishmael to the wilderness of Beer-sheba. Traditionally it is Sarah's intolerable abuse of Hagar that forces the slave to flee with her son. However, Sarah's action, with the God's approval, results not from an emotional state but from adherence to a form of legalistic tradition.

An astonishing amount of distortion has been built into Genesis by the authors of the narratives, whether intentionally or not, and the falsehoods and fantasies have since been propagated and perpetuated by preachers and scholars. The following chapters attempt to disclose how this was done, particularly where women are concerned.

I

SARAH AS SISTER AND WIFE

Sexual relations between close relatives occur twice in the Genesis narratives. Sarah and Abram were husband and wife, but they were also, in patrilineal terms, sister and brother because they had the same father; no explanation is given in the text as to why Sarah was married to her brother. Their nephew Lot had sexual relations with his two daughters. The reasons given are that there were no other men for the daughters to conceive with, and Lot was drunk at the time. Leviticus 18:6 and 9, however, forbids these relationships. Leviticus 18 also forbids two sisters to marry the same man, but the sisters Leah and Rachel were married to Jacob. Why were so many such relationships acceptable at that time?

The question is resolved if all these people — Sarah and Abram; Leah, Rachel and Jacob; and Lot and his daughters — were functioning in a social system different from that of our patrilineal one, a system which described incest in different terms.

The Question of Incest

Incest is defined as copulation between blood relatives. Usually the sexual act of a woman with her brother, father, or uncle is described as incestuous, though some communities include first cousins, or even second or more distant cousins in the category of blood relations, and therefore marriage or sexual relationships are forbidden for them also. Incest is and has been an almost universal taboo.

Nevertheless, close relatives did marry in both Egypt and Mesopotamia. Sister–brother unions existed in mythology and in royal families in the ancient Near East, though not in the community at large. The pharaohs were married to the most suitable of their sisters, half-sisters, or cousins. The religious reason for this was the union of the

6

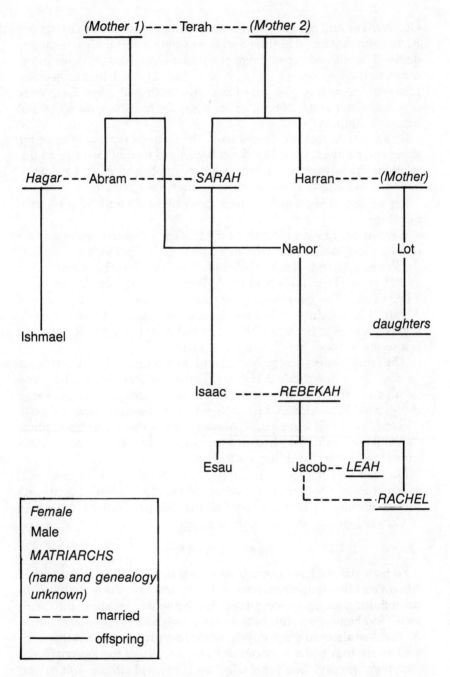

Table 1. Genealogy of Characters Mentioned in Chapter I

Goddess Isis and her brother, the God Osiris. In Sumerian mythology Kishar and Anshar, daughter and son of the powerful Mesopotamian deities Ti'amat and Apsu, were married and had a son, Anu. In Semitic mythology the Goddess Anath was married to her brother. However, according to Cyrus Gordon, Anath and Aliyn Ba'al were only half-sister and half-brother because they had the same father but different mothers.[3]

Sarah and Abram are described in the Genesis narratives as being sister and brother. Their blood relationship is exactly the same as the relationship between the Ugaritic deities Anath and Aliyn Ba'al: they have the same father but different mothers (see Table 1).

Let us review the stories which describe Sarah and Abram's relationship.

Genesis 11, 12, and 13[4] give us the biblical account of the migration of Sarah and Abram from Ur in southern Mesopotamia to Canaan, the Promised Land. Terah, Abram's father, has two other sons: Nahor and Harran. Harran has died in Ur, leaving a son, Lot. Abram has a wife, Sarah. The people who migrate from Ur are Terah, his son Abram, his daughter-in-law Sarah, and his grandson Lot. No mention is made as to the whereabouts of Nahor at this time. A comment is also made about Sarah: she has no child.

The family leaves Ur (*see* Map I) and travels up the Euphrates River to a northern town called Haran. They settle there for a while, and Terah dies. The story continues with Abram getting a message from a deity called El Shaddai, who tells him to leave his homeland and go to "a land that I will show you." Abram takes his wife and his nephew "and all the wealth they had amassed and all the persons they had acquired in Haran," and they go to Canaan.

On their way through Canaan (*see* Map II) the group stops at local sanctuaries at Shechem and Bethel, where Abram builds altars. As they continue their journey they find that there is drought in the land of Canaan, so they go on south to Egypt.

Sarah and the Kings

So far what we have learned about Sarah is that she is the wife of Abram and the daughter-in-law of Terah, and that she is childless. In the following sequence we get our first personal glimpse of the matriarch. The biblical account tells a very strange story. It goes like this: As they are about to enter Egypt, Abram says to his wife Sarah, "I am well aware that you are a beautiful woman. When the Egyptians see you, they will say, 'She is his wife,' and they will kill me, and let you live. Say then that you are my sister, that it may go well with me because of you, and that I may remain alive thanks to you." As they enter Egypt, Pharaoh's courtiers praise Sarah to Pharaoh and she is taken to his palace.

This part of the story implies two things: (a) that Sarah agreed to say she was Abram's sister, and (b) that she agreed to become Pharaoh's mistress. Because of this, the story continues, things went well with Abram; he acquired sheep, oxen, asses, male and female slaves, she-asses, and camels. But also because of this, "the Lord" afflicted Pharaoh and his household with mighty plagues. Pharaoh sent for Abram and said, "See what you have done to me. Why did you not tell me that she was your wife? Now here is your wife, take her and be gone." And Pharaoh put men in charge of Abram and sent him away.

This basic story is repeated three times in Genesis, with a change of characters and details. The first, as we have seen, involves Sarah, Abram, and Pharaoh; the second also includes Sarah and Abram, but with Abimelech, ruler of Gerar (*see* Map II). The third tells of Rebekah and Isaac with Abimelech. In each sequence, the husband begs the wife to say that she is his sister so that his life may be spared. This does not seem to say much for the character of the patriarchs. Would they really have allowed their wives to be "taken" by kings even at the risk of losing their lives? What induced the kings to give Abram recompense after he had deceived them? Were Sarah and Rebekah so submissive to their husbands that they would go along with such a scheme without objection? We will come back to these episodes many times in the next chapters. Their meaning will be much clearer when we view them in a perspective different from the traditional one. Biblical scholarship customarily tends to evade the issue of the morality of the patriarchs and instead concentrates on the so-called sister–wife motif. More to the point is the sister–brother theme, which has not, to my knowledge, been satisfactorily explained.

Whatever the original story, whatever the source of the Genesis narratives, it is important to remember that the theme has been interpreted and reinterpreted many times throughout the ages. The original material was handed down from generation to generation in the form of oral tradition. Then at some point a version of the story was transcribed by ancient redactors or scribes, each editing according to a personal set of rules and regulations.

Since that early recording, biblical commentators through the ages have made an effort to explain the discrepancies found in the texts. Incest, we know, has been an almost universal taboo, except where royalty is concerned, as in Egypt. Yet Abram, in an exchange with Abimelech, tells the king that Sarah "is indeed my sister, my father's

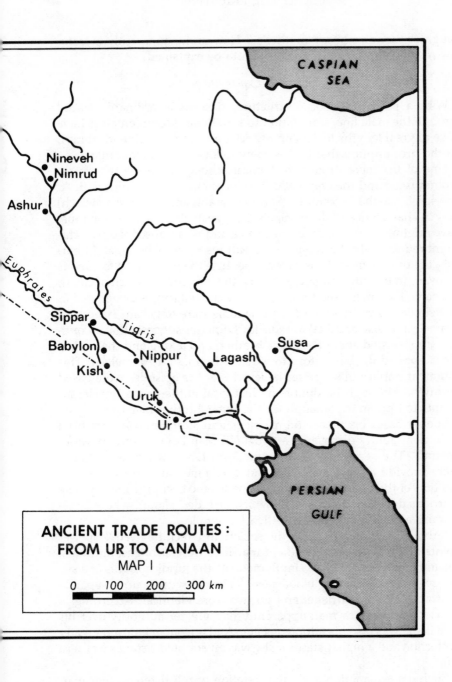

CASPIAN
SEA

Nineveh
Nimrud

Ashur

Euphrates

Sippar
Tigris

Babylon
Nippur
Lagash
Susa

Kish

Uruk

Ur

PERSIAN

GULF

ANCIENT TRADE ROUTES :
FROM UR TO CANAAN
MAP I

0   100   200   300 km

daughter though not my mother's." How is the apparently incestuous relationship of Sarah and Abram to be explained?

Patriarchal Explanations

With a patriarchal social structure, descent is ordinarily traced through the male line, from father to son. Biblical commentators have gone to great lengths to explain the relationship of Sarah and Abram, on the presumption that their society followed patriarchal rules.

One of the most prominent biblical scholars to tackle the sister–brother issue and the enigmatic story of Sarah and the kings is E. A. Speiser. Since the two stories (Sarah–Pharaoh and Sarah–Abimelech) vary in characters and detail, Speiser suggests that each version must have originated from a different source and was transcribed by a different redactor.[5] In the version that features Sarah, Abram, and Pharaoh, the unknown scribe is called J. because the name used for God is Jehovah. In the other source, in which the king is Abimelech of Gerar, the name Elohim is used for the deity, so the redactor is designated E. The similar story in which the protagonists are Rebekah, Isaac, and Abimelech is also ascribed to redactor J. Speiser suggests that an original story existed about a sister, a brother, and a king and that redactor E. applied the basic story to Sarah, Abram, and Abimelech. This comment implies that Speiser believed that the episodes were based on myth. Although he doubts its historical authenticity, Speiser attempts to find an explanation for the sister–brother marriage.

Speiser bases his theory on marriage and adoption contracts from an ancient library discovered at Nuzi (*see* Map IV) in northern Mesopotamia. The several thousand cuneiform tables which were found there provide a vivid and many-sided commentary on the life and customs of the people known as Hurrians who occupied the city. The Hurrians dominated a vast area which included Haran, where Terah (Sarah's and Abram's father) settled for awhile.

"Abram was influenced by the society in which he lived," Speiser points out,[6] "where the bonds of marriage were strongest and most solemn when the wife had simultaneously the juridical status of a sister, regardless of actual blood ties."[7] Hurrians drew up a separate contract for each marriage, and no two were identical. According to Speiser's research, a man apparently had greater authority over his wife if she was also his adopted sister. And a woman enjoyed greater protection and a higher status if she was an adopted sister as well as a wife.

Speiser's explanation and interpretation of the sister–brother marriage theme is typical of much of biblical scholarship in its attitude toward women. The purpose of marriage in the ancient Near East, he

12

comments, was to provide an heir, and the higher the status of the mother, the higher the status of the heir. "The purity of the content [was] protected by the quality of the container," as Speiser so deftly puts it.[8] The higher status of sistership improved the "container" (Sarah), giving the wife of the patriarch (Abram) the "quality" required to produce the subsequent generation (Isaac). Rebekah is also the beneficiary of improved status when she is introduced to Abimelech as the sister of Isaac.

Speiser continues: "Both Abram and Isaac were married to women who enjoyed a privileged status." It was "that kind of distinction that may well have been worthy of emphasis in the presence of their royal hosts, since it enhanced the credentials of the visitors. Status has always played a role in international relations, as far back as available records can take us."[9]

Thus, Speiser suggests that the biblical women may have been adopted by their husbands to raise their status. However, the biblical text explicitly states that Sarah and Abram were brother and sister but that Rebekah and Isaac were *not*; the adoption contracts cannot apply to both couples. Why would a brother want to adopt his own sister?

On the basis of the Nuzi documents, Speiser gives the matriarchs high status without allowing the women any merit in this status, since it was granted by the adoptive action of their husbands. He further deprives the matriarchs of their real condition as mothers and women by his unique interpretation of the adoptive sisterhood position; he views the matriarchs as merely improved containers in which to produce high-quality successors to the patriarchs. Speiser's theory, however, has been disputed on the grounds that the Nuzi documents emphasize an originally *low* status of the women involved.[10] Of the thirteen tablets then available to him, Speiser chose only one to use as evidence for his hypothesis; and even in that one, the girl who was adopted as sister had originally been a slave. Apart from that, in almost all of the sister-adoption documents, the adoptive brother "announces his intention to marry his new sister off to another man, to receive the bride-price."[11] In other words, it seems that recorded Hurrian adoptions were more related to business than to status. A man's adoption of a woman as sister was not for the woman's sake, but was a way for the man to get a good price for her. Presumably, an adopted sister brought a better price than a slave.

Alternative Kinship Systems and Matrilineal Categories

At the beginning of this chapter incest was defined as being a sexual relationship between blood relatives. We must now go a step further and describe the categories we are discussing.

brother — son of same mother and father or mother or father
father — mate of mother (generally) and progenitor of the offspring
uncle — father's brother or mother's brother

The kinship terms we have just described are patrilineal, of course, where descent is traced through the male. In a matrilineal kinship system, descent is traced through the female. Although descent can only be traced through either the female or male line, innumerable kinship patterns are possible. That some of these patterns are present in Genesis can, I believe, be deduced from the narratives.

In Genesis, Sarah is initially presented to us as Terah's daughter-in-law, wife of his son Abram. There is absolutely no suggestion that a blood tie exists between Terah and Sarah. However, much later on in the text Abram explains his relationship to Sarah like this: "She is indeed my sister, my father's daughter but not my mother's." (Gen. 20:12)

This revelation leads us to many questions. What social order was Abram following? What was Sarah dealing with? And what did the redactors think of it all?

For the kings, to whom patriliny was the norm, descent was traced through the male line, so Sarah and Abram, both being the offspring of one father, Terah, are brother and sister. In Sarah's society, however, patriliny was not the custom. Sarah is introduced to us as Terah's daughter-in-law, not as his daughter. In matriliny, descent is traced through the mother; and since, as Abram explained, he and Sarah had different mothers, they would not be considered siblings, or in any way blood relatives. It is for this reason that they were permitted to be married.

Considering the different views of offspring in matriliny and patriliny, what was the sense of the exchange between Abram and the kings?

Abram: In your society, Sarah is regarded as my sister and therefore our union is not valid in your eyes. As my sister, Sarah is free to become your wife.

The king: In your society, Sarah is not your sister and your union is valid. Why did you pretend that you were following a patrilineal system? I took her as my wife because you said she was your sister, and I believed you. Furthermore, this action of mine is a religious and political offense to your deity and your nation. This was not my intention.

> Here, take back your wife and be gone. But take also
> these gifts [sheep, oxen, etc. (Pharaoh); a thousand
> shekels of silver (Abimelech)]. Take them to appease
> your deities and as an expression of good faith that it
> was not my intention to offer disrespect or insult to the
> customs of a neighboring nation.

In all this it would seem that Sarah was passed back and forth from one man to the other without a word, like the passive patriarchal wife she is supposed to be, with no feelings or rights of her own. We will see, in later chapters, that this was not the case at all.

Matriliny often disregarded the biological function of the father, and children of the same father but of different mothers would not be regarded as siblings. Sarah is introduced in Genesis as "Terah's daughter-in-law, the wife of his son Abram," as though she were not related by blood to either Terah or Abram. Was Terah's biological function not acknowledged by Sarah's family? Did Terah regard Abram as his son but not Sarah as his (blood relative) daughter?

The sister–brother relationship of Sarah and Abram has been explained away by scholars who interpreted the term "sister" to mean niece or adopted sister, although the text explicitly states that Sarah is the daughter of Terah, but has a mother different from Abram's. It seems these biblical scholars are either ignorant of or unwilling to accept the relationship of Sarah and Abram described by the original authors of Genesis and retained by scribes recording the stories at a later time. The scribes must have been familiar with the matrilineal social structure of the period of the stories — a period in which the union of nonuterine siblings was not regarded as incestuous. At a later time, in a more stringent patriarchal setting, Sarah's double relationship to Abram became difficult to explain.

Thus we can see sister–brother marriage is quite understandable in a female-oriented society if the siblings have the same father but not the same mother, as was the case with Sarah and Abram. Incest taboos exist, but close relationships are defined differently than in our society because family relationships are traced through the mother alone.

Genesis and Mythology

T. J. Meek, in his book *Hebrew Origins,* traces ancestor worship among the early Hebrews from primitive animism to the cult of the dead. Family worship of the dead led to clan worship of ancestral heroes: "Abram, Isaac and Jacob became eponymous heroes to the Hebrews. Their graves were shrines where there were rites of worship," he says.[12] Indeed, some of those graves are shrines even now. (I saw Arab women and men praying at Rachel's tomb after the Six-Day War in Israel, hoping that she could return Jerusalem to them.)

It is possible that in late Israelite tradition Sarah and Abram had become not only ancestors to be worshipped by their descendants but also mythical figures who shared some of the characteristics of local deities. One of the more familiar attributes of semi-divine beings in myth is unusual longevity. In the ancient Near East, kings were said to have reigned for hundreds of years. The Babylonian hero Gilgamesh is recorded as reigning for 126 years. Of the biblical characters of great age, Methuselah and Noah are perhaps the most well-known. As the stories get nearer to historical times the length of life is reduced to more reasonable dimensions. Sarah is supposed to have lived 127 years and Abram 175, as compared to Methuselah's 969 and Noah's 950.

It is interesting to note, however, that the descendants of Shem (Noah's son), who lived to between 200 and 400 years of age, are reported to have "begotten" their sons at the more customary ages of 29 to 40. If living to an unusual age implies a semi-divine category, the birth of a first child to parents of advanced age must suggest a most prodigious event. Abram was 76 when Ishmael was born, and Sarah is the only woman in the Bible whose advanced age (90) is recorded when her son Isaac was conceived.

The stories of semi-divine beings, however, originate in the remote past of pre-history, a period in which the social structure may have differed from that of the historical past. Matriliny was evidently characteristic of some ancient societies (and will be examined in greater detail in subsequent chapters).

I believe that it is necessary to consider the concept of the semi-divine with relation to the characters portrayed in the Genesis narratives. The argument is developed further in chapters VII and VIII. (1) Sarah was married to her (half-)brother at a time when the marriage of (royal or) semi-divine siblings was acceptable. (2) This may have facilitated ancestor worship among the early Hebrews or Israelites, at least in the case of Sarah and Abram. (3) Later, when the oral tradition on which the biblical texts were based was transcribed, ancestor worship was no longer acceptable, and the semi-divine aspect of the ancestors was greatly reduced. The question of incest became a problem that had to be dealt with. The repetition of the sister–brother theme three times lends a saga-like tone to the narratives, giving the effect that the stories are closer to myth than reality.

The narratives with supernatural connotations have thus evolved through three stages:

1. the original story, or actual event
2. the original story elaborated with supernatural themes pertaining to ancestor worship (mostly in oral transmission)
3. a toning down (by later scribes) of the semi-divine aspects in the written version of the narratives

An understanding of the three stages of development in the Genesis narratives is imperative to an in-depth analysis, particularly in those portions of the text in which vestiges of supernatural themes remain. (We will review these three stages later, in chapter VII.) The original story or actual event, which contained a matrilineal element, did not contain elements of ancestor worship. Then in some portions of the text, influenced by the stage of oral transmission in which ancestor worship was acceptable, the original events were seen in terms of the semi-divine: the marriage of sister and brother was one of these.

Finally, in the third stage, the supernatural character of the ancestors was toned down by the scribes; that is, they chose to emphasize certain portions and perhaps forget others, according to the needs of the times. In this category we can also include all subsequent scholars who, through emphasis and interpretation, have obscured the original story or event by emphasizing the roles and activities of the males while minimizing those of the women.

At some point the biblical texts were declared holy scriptures, and tampering with the word of God was forbidden while traces of the original stories still remained. As a result, many enigmatic passages still appear in our sacred scriptures. These mysterious passages have never been successfully explained because they have been approached only by men with a completely male-oriented patriarchal attitude. (Speiser is a good example.) It is nevertheless possible to reevaluate the texts by focusing on the women rather than on the men, and to find, perhaps to our surprise, that the supposedly difficult passages are not so mysterious.

It would seem that Leviticus (the book of the law expounded by Levite priests) was in part a set of regulations that aimed at changing the concept of close relationships. In Sarah's system, Terah was acknowledged as her social father, but his biological function was not recognized. In other words, in Sarah's society it was descent through the mother that counted, not through the father; family members consisted of a mother, her mother, her sisters and brothers, and her children. The Levite priests, addressing the men in the community, were later to impose a reformation redefining the concept of incest to include the biological recognition of the father. Leviticus 18 reads like a manual for the teaching of a new ethic which consolidates the father's position in the group that is now known as the nuclear family. "The nakedness of your sister, *your father's daughter* or your mother's, whether born into the household *or outside,* you shall not uncover" (v.9) and "The nakedness of your *father's wife's daughter,* who was born into your father's household, she is your sister, do not uncover her nakedness" (v.11) are teachings which reflect a fundamental change from the matrilineal social order observed by Sarah and Abram.

II

FROM UR TO HEBRON, CITY OF SARAH

The redactors and scribes of Genesis carefully recorded the names of certain towns, cities, and geographic locations, which they evidently considered to be important. Some of the names of these places, like Mamre (*see* Map II), have been changed, or their locations have been forgotten; some, like Hebron, remain unchanged; and others, such as Ur of the Chaldees, identify present archeological sites.

The three sites just mentioned — Ur, Hebron, and Mamre — are linked to Abram by biblical commentators. Abram, they contend, was born in Ur (although there is some controversy about that); he and his father Terah left Ur to go to Canaan, but stayed in Haran where Terah died and Abram got the calling "to the land that I will show you"; and finally, Abram "dwelt at the terebinths [sacred groves] of Mamre which are in Hebron." The biblical texts do give us this information, but they also note that these were places in which Sarah lived.

I believe, and hope to show convincingly, that Ur was Sarah's birthplace, not Abram's; that Terah took his family to Haran because of Sarah; and that Mamre at Hebron was always the residence of Sarah when they were in Canaan, but not always that of Abram. The sanctity of the terebinth grove was relevant to Sarah, and to her life.

Another locale of great importance in the story of Sarah is the cave of Machpelah, where only Sarah, her husband, and her successors were buried. A whole chapter in Genesis is dedicated to the description of the matriarch's burial site: "Ephron's land in Machpelah, facing Mamre — the field with its cave and all the trees anywhere within the confines of that field." A detailed account is given of the transaction between Abram and Ephron, owner of the land, which was witnessed by the elders of the town, "the children of Heth."

19

Before continuing with the remarkable events in the matriarch's life, I will give some description of Sarah's birthplace and places of residence, and explain why these places should be associated with Sarah rather than with Abram, why they are more important to her story than to his. Since this book is primarily about Sarah, the names Ur, Haran, and Mamre will come up time and again and will become as meaningful to the reader as the name Sarah itself.

From Ur to Haran (Gen. 11:26-32)

Ur of the Chaldees, a city-state on the Euphrates River in southern Mesopotamia (present day Iraq), is mentioned in the Bible as being the place from which Terah and his family emigrated. The implication is that Terah and his family — Abram, Sarah, and Lot — had lived in Ur and were now leaving. (Harran, Lot's father, had died in Ur.) Terah's intent was to go to Canaan, we are told; but when the family came to Haran, they settled there.

Seemingly, there is nothing out of the ordinary in this biblical statement; but the city of Haran is not located along the route to Canaan. The trade route that should have taken Terah and his family to Canaan followed the Euphrates River in a northerly direction from Ur to Terqa (in the vicinity of the famous city of Mari), from there in a southwesterly direction to Damascus in Syria, and then south to Canaan (*see* Map I). Instead, however, Terah continued his journey north of Terqa along the Euphrates to the city of Haran on the Balikh River. What could have been the reason for Terah's indirect route?

Other queries also come to mind. Were Terah and his family natives of Ur in southern Mesopotamia? Various passages in Genesis point to Haran and an unidentified place called Nahor, towns in the north, as the home of Abram. I suggest that Abram did come from the north and that Ur of the Chaldees was possibly the birthplace of Sarah. Patriarchal tradition assumed a connection between Abram and Ur simply because Ur is mentioned in Genesis. Emphasis on males rather than females made it inconceivable to ancient as well as to later scholars that the name of the city of Ur may have been recorded originally only in relation to the matriarch Sarah — even though Genesis 24:7 and various other passages designate the north as being Abram's homeland and despite the notable absence of information concerning Sarah's background.

It is certainly possible that much of Sarah's story was erased or obliterated as time went on but that occasional evidence remained, such as the mention in the texts of Ur of the Chaldees. As Sarah's importance decreased in the stories, some explanation had to be found for this evidence, and since Abram had become the principal character, the city of Ur became accepted as his birthplace.

When scholars became aware of the contradiction, that both Ur in the south and the area of Haran in the north were assumed to be Abram's birthplace, they tried to solve the dilemma.

The Two Cities of Ur

It has been argued by Cyrus Gordon and W. F. Albright, for instance, that Ur and Haran are mentioned in connection with Abram because they were both trade centers.[13] Gordon finds evidence in a tablet from Ugarit (Syria) that Hittite merchants were restricted from buying real estate in Ugarit, and that these Hittite merchants are from a city by the name of Ura, somewhere in northern Mesopotamia. Gordon contends that this evidence implies that the patriarchal family did not originate in the southern Sumerian city-state of Ur of the Chaldees as stated in Genesis. Indeed, a tablet recently found in the ancient city of Ebla (Tell Mardikh) does, according to a lecture given by Giovanni Pettinato, mention a city of Ur in the region of Haran. In my opinion, however, this discovery confirms the report in Genesis that Terah's family came from Ur in the south (later, in the first millennium B.C.E., known as Chaldea), rather than the city of Ur(a) in the northern region. Although the name Chaldea was eventually used for the whole of Babylonia, it seems obvious that the biblical scribes were being precise about which of the two cities of the same name the patriarchs originally set out from: not from Ur in the region of Haran, but *Ur of the Chaldees* in the south. The patriarchal family is seen, then, as taking part in a migration from Ur in the south to the "Caravan City" Haran in the north, and then on to Canaan and Egypt.[14]

One of the northern place-names associated with the patriarchs is Aram-Naharaim (Aram of the rivers), mentioned in Genesis 24:4, 10 — an area in northern Mesopotamia (*see* Map III), in which a city called Nahor (not clearly identified geographically but which could coincide with Nahur of the Mari Texts), situated east of the upper Balikh River, is given as the birthplace of Abram: "on the other side of the flood [i.e., river]," in Joshua 24:2. Haran was the city located in the area of Paddan-Aram to which Terah and his family migrated from Ur. This area was the home of Rebekah, Leah, and Rachel, and their respective fathers, Bethuel and Laban, who are characterized as Arameans.[15]

Although Abram's birthplace is understood to be in the north, Harran, another of Terah's sons, was born and died in Ur in the south (Gen. 11:28). Possibly Abram's mother was a northerner and Harran's

21

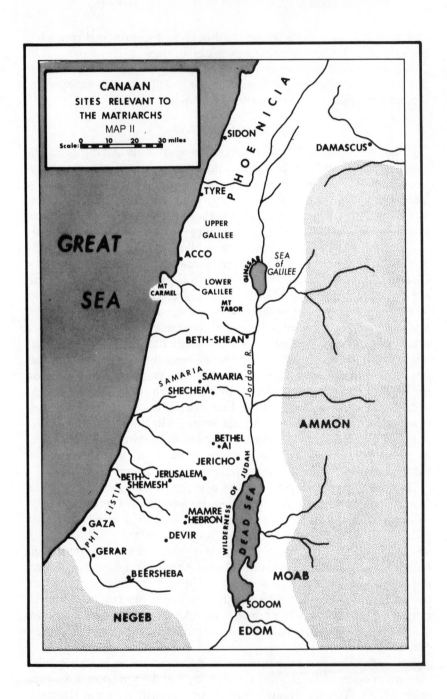

CANAAN
SITES RELEVANT TO
THE MATRIARCHS
MAP II
Scale: 0 10 20 30 miles

PHOENICIA

GREAT

SEA

SIDON
DAMASCUS
TYRE
UPPER
GALILEE
ACCO
GINESAR
SEA of GALILEE
MT CARMEL
LOWER GALILEE
MT TABOR
BETH-SHEAN
Jordan R.
SAMARIA
SAMARIA
SHECHEM
AMMON
BETHEL
AI
JERICHO
JUDAH
BETH-SHEMESH
JERUSALEM
WILDERNESS OF
PHILISTIA
MAMRE
HEBRON
GAZA
DEAD SEA
DEVIR
GERAR
BEERSHEBA
MOAB
SODOM
NEGEB
EDOM

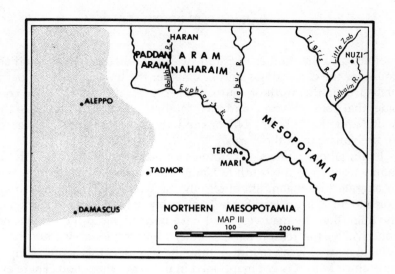

NORTHERN MESOPOTAMIA

MAP III

0   100   200 km

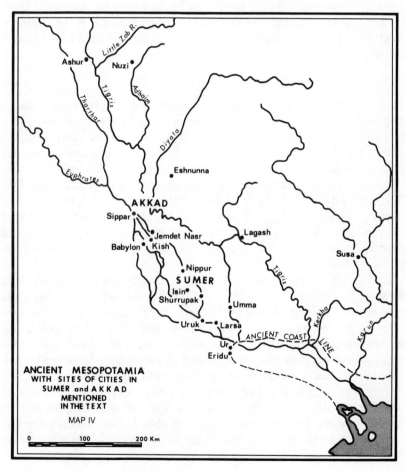

ANCIENT MESOPOTAMIA
WITH SITES OF CITIES IN
SUMER and AKKAD
MENTIONED
IN THE TEXT

MAP IV

0   100   200 Km

mother, also the mother of Sarah, was a southerner. This would account for the conflicting views of whether the homeland of the patriarchs was in the north or south.[16] It is conceivable, therefore, to consider that Sarah, Harran, and their mother[17] were natives of Ur in the south and that Abram, Nahor, and their mother were natives of Aram-Naharaim in the north.

Terah, whose name also connotes a northern city, moved with his family from Ur in the south to Haran in the north. His intention was to migrate to Canaan, although why he would have traveled so far north to do so is unclear. Since Terah's son Nahor is not mentioned in the migration, he may very well have been living in the north, and conceivably, the reason for his father's lengthy journey could have been to marry Milcah to him — though, of course, this is pure conjecture, since Milcah is not mentioned in the Terah migration. There are many other possibilities for the move. Historically, Ur suffered a long spell of upheavals, pointing to a political reason for the emigration; or Terah could have originally moved from Haran to Ur and was now moving back.

Ancient Near Eastern Goddesses

Ur, the city-state from which Terah migrated with his family, had a population of about 200,000 inhabitants in 2000 B.C.E. Each city in Sumer (*see* Map IV) was under the protection of a patron deity, and the patron deity of Ur was the moon-God Nanna. Nanna was sometimes known as Sin, a name possibly of Semitic origin. Nanna's wife was the lunar Goddess Ningal, known in Ugaritic literature as Nikkal. Unlike most Sumero-Akkadian deities, Nikkal was also revered in Canaan, as well as in Ugarit.[18] The daughter of Ningal and Nanna was the powerful Goddess Inanna, patron goddess of the ancient cities of Kish and Erech, who in early Sumerian times had been the patron deity of Aratta.

Let us digress somewhat from the description of the city of Ur to look at a few interesting features about the goddesses. To the Semites, Inanna was known as Ishtar. Pictures of Mesopotamian goddesses were impressed on pottery plaques; they were the prototypes of those in Palestine, most of which show the nude figure of the Goddess Astarte. These plaques (*see* Plates 2 and 3), according to Albright, are among the most common religious objects discovered in the late Bronze Age (21st to 13th centuries B.C.E.) levels in Palestine.[19] Plaques of Astarte, who is identified with the Canaanite Anath, were also found to be the most common religious objects found by Albright in the biblical town of Devir, southwest of Hebron (*see* Map II). Devir (the site known as Tell Beit Mirsim) is also the biblical term for the Holy of Holies of the Jerusalem Temple,[20] and the ancient name of that town was Kiriath-Sepher, the "Book City." Sarah the matriarch, as we shall see, lived and died in Kiriath-Arba, later called Hebron — close to the Book City where Astarte was venerated.

During his excavations at Ur, Sir C. Leonard Woolley found plaques and figurines in the ruins of houses and in graves similar to those discovered at Kiriath-Sepher. But the city of Ur was no small town like the Book City. It had an extensive sacred area known as the *temenu*, which consisted of Ur's main temples, a ziggurat (stepped pyramid), and the building which housed the *ens* (high priests and priestesses) and the *naditu*, priestesses who were cloistered. (The *naditu* at times lived in the cloister, at least in the early years of their service.)[21] Women *ens* served gods, and men served goddesses.[22] At the Ekishnugal, as the *temenu* of Ur was called, the *en* was a woman who served the patron deity named Nanna-Sin, and who, in certain rituals, represented the Goddess Ningal.

Haran, like Ur, was a great trading center; but it also had the distinction of beng a center of moon veneration, and its patron deity was the same as Ur's: Nanna-Sin, the moon-god. We cannot discount the possibility that Terah moved from Ur to Haran because the northern city was the only other locale in Mesopotamia that was a center of moon worship and whose patron deities were Nanna-Sin and Ningal. Albright and others maintain that the migration of Terah's family was for business purposes, and that Haran and most of the sites visited by Abram were trading centers. But why would we be told about the patriarch's business stops if the story of Genesis concerns the beginnings of a faith? Obviously, the patriarchs must have had some form of making a livelihood, and Abram's may have involved trading; he had amassed considerable wealth in Haran. Nevertheless, on the way to Mamre, the sacred area near Hebron, the patriarch built altars at Shechem and the hill country between Ai and Bethel, already ancient religious centers at that time (*see* Map II). Therefore, the reason for the emigration from Ur to Haran must have been for religious purposes as well as for business. Our interest in this question is, of course, how much the choice of locale may have concerned the matriarch Sarah. As we follow the story of our protagonists we will find that the abodes of Abram were not necessarily those of Sarah; all the places where Sarah lived were exclusively associated with religion, whereas those of Abram were also associated with trade.

The name of the area where Sarah lived most of her life was Kiriath-Arba (Gen. 23:1), but by the time her life was recorded the name of

The forms of Goddesses were impressed on pottery plaques.

PLATES 2 and 3. Pottery plaques from Beth Shemesh,

26

These Astarte plaques are among the most common religious objects discovered. Israel. *(The University Museum, University of Pennsylvania.)*

27

that area had been changed to Hebron. The Bible always refers to the town by its later name, Hebron, just as it indicates that Ur is *of the Chaldees*, so that readers of the texts could easily identify the places. Present-day Hebron is close enough to where ancient Kiriath-Arba is supposed to have been that we too can continue to call Sarah's place of residence by its present name.

Abram's Choice

When Sarah and Abram left Mesopotamia, they took with them Harran's son Lot. "Abram went forth as the Lord had spoken to him, and Lot went with him." (Gen. 12:4) Lot also went with Sarah and Abram to Egypt, but he did not play a part in the strange incident with the Pharaoh. "From Egypt, Abram went up into the Negeb, with his wife and all that he possessed, together with Lot" (Gen. 13:1).

Lot, like Abram, also had "flocks and tents and herds"; "their possessions were so great that they could not stay together." There was quarreling among their herdsmen. Abram suggested that they separate and that Lot choose from the land before them where he would like to settle so that there should be no strife between them: "If you go north, I will go south, and if you go south, I will go north." Biblical commentators have seen in this incident an example of the magnanimous character of the patriarch.[23] He gave Lot the choice, and his nephew chose the whole plain of the Jordan, pitching his tents near Sodom, south of the Dead Sea (*see* Map II).

"And Abram," the text continiues, "moved his tent and came to dwell at the terebinths of Mamre which are in Hebron," about fifty miles northwest of the location chosen by Lot.

I do not want to minimize a possible magnanimous trait in the patriarch's character; but "The Lord said to Abram, after Lot had parted from him, 'Raise your eyes and look out from where you are, to the north and the south, to the east and west, for I give all the land that you see to you and your offspring forever.' "

Why did Abram choose the sacred grove of Mamre? Was this the most convenient place he could find for his flocks and herds and tents and herdsmen? As the story unfolds, I think it will become apparent that Mamre at Hebron was chosen by Abram as the residence of Sarah. Barring one visit to the king of Gerar, Sarah spent the rest of her life in the vicinity of Hebron.

Theophany at Mamre

The episode most indicative of the significance of Mamre during Sarah's lifetime is that of supernatural visitation and communication at that site. The main theme of Genesis 18 describes the visit of two angels and a deity who bring the promise of a son to Sarah.

The consecrated character of the terebinth grove is highlighted not only by the sanctity of the woman who lives there but also by the nature of her visitors. As far as we know from the texts, the visitors are the only ones who visit Mamre or with whom Sarah has any interchange or communication, apart from her family and attendants. Even in this sequence most of the conversation takes place between Abram and the visitors; but this may be due to later editing.

The preceding chapter, Genesis 17, is a masterpiece of subtlety. Without diminishing the stature of the patriarch — who is obviously content with his offspring Ishmael, and is blessed by El Shaddai with a promise of twelve princes as progeny — a covenant is made with Sarah. Both Hagar's son Ishmael and Sarah's future son Isaac are given the assurance of descendants by the deity. Abram will be the father of princes, while rulers of people will issue from Sarah. This is not a contest in the number of progeny: both Sarah and Abram's descendants will become nations. The important issue is the quality of the covenant with those descendants — a spiritual quality that is generally a matter of religion and religious ritual.

This sequence of promises to Abram was probably not received by the patriarch at Mamre, since the covenant included circumcision and Abram "took his son Ishmael, and all his homeborn slaves and all those he had bought, every male among Abram's retainers, and he circumcised the flesh of their foreskins on that very day, as God had spoken to him."

Genesis 18 and the story of the heavenly visitors is but another version of the same subject. Written by *J.*, it is considered to be from an earlier source than Genesis 17. In the older version there is no mention of Ishmael, and Sarah laughs unbelievingly: "Shall I in truth bear a child, old as I am?" In *P.* (the priestly tradition), it is Abram who laughs: "Can a child be born to a man a hundred years old, or can Sarah bear a child at ninety?" It would seem that the later redactors were trying to condition their readers to the fatherhood of Abram, whereas the older version strongly implied divine intervention in the conception of Isaac. In either case, the main theme remains the promise of a son to Sarah, and Mamre is the hallowed ground on which this promise is given. It is in Mamre that Sarah conceives and gives birth to Isaac. I will deal with the circumstances surrounding this mysterious conception in Part Two.

Fourteen years passed after Ishmael's birth before Sarah was able to fulfill her desire to have an heir of her own. The matriarch's disaccord with Hagar had forced her to reject Ishmael as her son. But Sarah's problems with Hagar and Ishmael were not resolved with the birth of Isaac. Sarah, as we shall see, was forced to banish the slave and her son.

Abram is thus forced to witness the exile of his concubine Hagar and his beloved son Ishmael; but this does not mean that the patriarch is prevented from being with them. Immediately after Hagar and Ishmael are sent to wander in the wilderness of Beer-sheba, we find Abram there also, conducting negotiations with Abimelech of Gerar and planting a tamarisk at Beer-sheba. The text also states that Abram "resided in the land of the Philistines" a long time. (Gen. 21:34)

Abram then continued to spend most of his time away from Hebron. No mention is made of Sarah. It would seem that she continued to live, and eventually die, in Mamre. If Sarah was with Abram, why did she die in Hebron? There is no mention of Abram returning to Hebron to live. He is there only to bury his wife, an important event which is described in minute detail.

Hebron must be remembered in terms of Sarah's life and death. How much importance her association with Hebron influenced its destiny is uncertain, but it will be remembered that Hebron remained the foremost religious center of the Hebrews and the early Israelites until David removed its influence to Jerusalem, which later became known as the City of David. Of all the places associated with the matriarch, Hebron at least should carry the affix "City of Sarah."

III

THE MATRIARCHS' AUTHORITY

In the preceding chapters we have seen that certain episodes in the Genesis narratives indicate that Sarah, Rebekah, and Rachel did not visualize themselves as belonging to a patrilineal descent group and were in fact endeavoring to maintain a matrilineal social structure. There is also evidence in these same episodes that the matriarchs were able to exert considerable authority in certain areas over family members, including their husbands.

In one instance, at least, Sarah relied on an ordinance known to us from a Mesopotamian stela with cuneiform inscription referred to as the Code of Hammurapi (*see* plates 4 and 5) number 147. In her dealings with her handmaid Hagar, Sarah obviously had the authority to invoke or abide by the legal system applicable in her homeland. By virtue of her power, Sarah, a stranger in a strange land, was also able to command the destinies of both Ishmael and Isaac. The matriarch's behavior was not that of a jealous or headstrong woman, as most biblical commentators have asserted in the past. On the contrary, she had good reason to proceed as she did.

The same can be said of Rebekah and Rachel. Their actions or reactions were not impulsive and willful ones. They too were struggling to maintain the social traditions to which they were accustomed, traditions they had brought with them from Mesopotamia to Canaan.

Furthermore, it will become apparent in the following pages that issues of a religious nature are touched upon in the stories of all three women. These incidents include Ishmael's "mocking" of Isaac, the blessing of Jacob, and Rachel's "theft" of the sacred images (*teraphim*).

Sarah's Heir

The very first verses in Genesis to tell us anything about the matriarch Sarah can be found in one of the famous lists of "begettings." It goes like this:

> This is the line of Terah:
> Terah begot Abram, Nahor, and Harran.
> And Harran begot Lot.
> Harran died in the lifetime of his father, Terah,
> in his native land, in Ur of the Chaldeans.
> Abram and Nahor took wives;
> the name of Abram's wife was Sarai,
> and that of Nahor's wife Milcah
> daughter of Harran, the father of Milcah and Iscah.
> Sarai was barren; she had no child.
>
> (Gen. 11:27-30)

What the Bible does not tell us in so many words is that Sarah was "barren" for close to thirty years! Later on in the stories, we hear that Sarah's daughter-in-law Rebekah and Rebekah's daughter-in-law Rachel were also "barren." Rebekah was childless for twenty years and Rachel for ten.

What seems most difficult to accept is that patriarchal men, whose aspirations are generally to have successors and heirs, would have stood by barren wives for decades without replacing them or taking second wives or concubines as was customary in those days. Abram did acquire a concubine, but only after he and Sarah had lived in Canaan for eleven years. They had been married in Ur and had also lived for some time in Haran, so Sarah and Abram had been together for about thirty years before the episode of the concubine. And according to the biblical account, the decision about the concubine was Sarah's, not Abram's.

Sarah had an Egyptian handmaid whose name was Hagar. Sarah said to Abram, "Consort with my maid; perhaps I shall have a son through her." Abram agrees and Hagar conceives. However, when Hagar "saw that she had conceived, her mistress was lowered in her esteem. Then Sarah treated her harshly and Hagar ran away from her." (Gen. 16:1-6)

This is the first of two episodes dealing with Sarah's conduct toward Hagar. However, these must be understood as two totally different problems, although they have often been quoted together to emphasize Sarah's cruelty to Hagar. I think it will become clear that the

matriarch was not personally cruel; she was simply following Mesopotamian law.

In the first episode, Sarah wanted a child, and urged Abram to co-
habit with Hagar for that purpose. But it is possible to interpret Sarah's story in quite a different light if we take into consideration the
traditions and customs of the times. It is also important to realize that
a misguided translation can make for a mistaken interpretation.

Take for instance the verse in which Sarah offers her husband her
handmaid: ". . . perhaps I shall have a son through her." A literal
translation of the Hebrew text is: ". . . that I shall be built up by
her."[24] The metaphor becomes clear when we know that "built up"
in this instance means lineage or succession. In this translation, Sarah
is not necessarily hoping to have a son; and she is indicating that her
intention is to regard the maid's child as *her* offspring, not her husband's.

Similar terminology is used in the famous Mesopotamian Code of
Hammurapi with regard to adoption: "If a man has taken an infant in
adoption for his sonship and has brought him up, *has built his house,*
and afterwards gets sons [of his own] and sets his face to expel the
adopted child, that son shall not then go destitute." This too is an
inexact translation. Literally, this Old Babylonian text reads "If a man
has taken an infant, has brought him up, made his house and afterwards gets sons, etc. [with him]."[25] Fathers did not build their sons
separate residences at that time; families lived together. For a man to
build a house for an adopted child does not make as much sense as
for him to bring up a child, "making his house" (i.e., lineage) with
that child. If he later gets sons of his own, conflicts could arise. This is
certainly the interpretation for an adoptive father who did not con-
template having, or who was unable to have, sons of the body, sons
of his own, at the time of the adoption. It is in this sense that Sarah
wishes to be "built up" by adopting Hagar's child as her own, whether by legal adoption or by implication.

Sarah Observes the Traditions of Her Homeland

According to later Jewish legend,[26] Hagar was the slave given to
Sarah by Pharaoh. As the property of Pharaoh, Hagar may very well
have been of higher than common rank. Whatever her origin, her
status is now reduced, and she is being used for a function of which
her mistress was incapable: to produce progeny. In this respect, Hagar is indisputably superior to her mistress. It seems only human that
she should take this opportunity to belittle Sarah — and she does.

PLATE 4. The stela of Hammurapi, erected in the Temple of the God Marduk in Babylon, ca. 1800 B.C.E.

PLATE 5. (right). Detail of the stela showing the cuneiform inscription, including regulations similar to those observed by Sarah. (*The Louvre, Cliché Musée Nationaux.*)

Because of this common human response, the law of Mesopotamia saw fit to regulate such situations. Paragraph 146 in the Hammurapi Code reads:

> If a man has married a priestess [of a certain rank] and she has given a slave girl to her husband and she bears sons, if (thereafter) that slave girl goes about making herself equal to her mistress, because she has borne sons, her mistress may not sell her; she may put the mark of a slave on her and count her with the slave girls. If she has not borne sons, her mistress may sell her.[27]

These regulations reflect precisely the situation in Genesis 16. Why has this amazing similarity not been noted by scholars? The most immediate response has been that this particular regulation applies to priestesses, and since the biblical texts refer to Sarah only as the wife of Abram, the regulation is assumed not to apply.[28] One scholar suggests that although the regulations specify *heirodules* ("priestesses"), it may be that they reflect a more general practice; in other words, he feels that Sarah could have been following the code as applying not only to priestesses but to any first wives.[29] But this suggestion is not legitimate. There is a distinct difference in the Code of Hammurapi between regulations for women of priestly rank and for first wives (sections 146–47 vs. 161–67, for instance).

Each verse in Genesis 16 corresponds to a paragraph in Hammurapi's Code. Let us compare the Code and the Bible.

CODE	GENESIS
1. If a priestess who is also a wife has given a slave girl to her husband.	1. So Sarai took her maid and gave her to her husband as concubine.
2. And she bears children.	2. And she conceived.
3. If thereafter the maid goes about making herself equal to her mistress . . .	3. Her mistress was lowered in her esteem.
4. Her mistress may not sell her . . .	4. Your maid is in your hands, deal with her as you think right.
5. She may put the mark (of a slave) on her.	5. Sarai treated her harshly.

In other words, Sarah gave her handmaid to Abram as a concubine, but when the woman showed disrespect to her mistress, she was treated harshly; that is, Hagar was reduced to the status of a slave. That Sarah chided her husband "The wrong done me is your fault!" implied that Abram had also behaved offensively to Sarah, perhaps in his attitude toward the concubine; but he can say nothing in Hagar's defense. Abram's "Deal with her as *you* think right" is recognition of Sarah's authority.

R. Patai, in *Sex and the Family in the Bible and the Middle East*, has a chapter on the powers of the patriarch in which he points out the unlimited authority the head of the family held over the life and death of his dependents, including his daughters, his sons, their wives, and their slaves.[30] But Abram did not have such authority over his wife or her maid. Abram is far from being the all-powerful patriarch he is reputed to be.

We have been told of Sarah's need or wish to have an heir(ess) and how she went about it. She acted in accordance with Mesopotamian rules which governed the conduct of women, not men. Those rules were not applicable to women who may have been barren but were specifically for women in particular religious groups who *were forbidden to have children of their own*. I believe that the matriarchs are to be seen as associated in some way with religious groups that observed such regulations, and that is why they are recorded as being barren. Obviously, the matriarchs were not barren; they all had children late in life. A more exact statement is that they initially remained childless. This fascinating issue will be covered in detail in Part Two. Here let us continue with the evidence of the matriarchs' authority, and how they used it to direct their own destinies and the destinies of their children.

Sarah and the "Mocking" Incident

Fourteen years have passed since Hagar conceived Ishmael, and now Sarah herself has a son, Isaac, who is old enough to be weaned. At a great feast arranged by Abram, Sarah saw "the son, whom Hagar the Egyptian had borne to Abram, playing. . . ." She said to Abram, "Cast out that slave-woman and her son, for the son of that slave shall not share in the inheritance with my son Isaac" (Gen. 21:9-10).

The biblical verb *(m)shq* used in this sentence is unclear and difficult to translate. It has been variously rendered "playing," "mocking," or "amusing." None of these terms, however, can justify Sarah's banishing Hagar and Ishmael from Hebron. The use of these terms give us the impression Ishmael was young and therefore blameless (he was about fifteen at the time), and that Sarah's action was due only to a mean and spiteful personality.

There are several questions to be considered in connection with this passage.

37

For one thing, there is a difference here with respect to the previous episode (Gen. 16) in which Sarah had requested Abram to "build up her house." Now Ishmael is referred to as Abram's son (Gen. 21:11). If Sarah had originally intended to regard her handmaid's issue as her own, when did Ishmael come to be considered Abram's son? As we have seen, Sarah's treatment of Hagar meant, in Hammurapi's terms, that she had "put the mark of a slave on her." Hagar has been demoted from handmaid or concubine to slave. If Hagar is now a slave, then her son Ishmael is the son of a slave, not a handmaid. In part this change of status could have disqualified him from becoming Sarah's son. Whatever the reason, Ishmael is now definitely identified as the son of the patriarch.

Another situation arises with regard to the implication in this verse that it is Abram, not Sarah, who has authority over Hagar. In the first episode Hagar is referred to as Sarah's handmaid (*shifhah*); now she is called bondswoman or slave (*amah*), having no rights of her own. Her son is the son of a slave (*ben-amah*). Abram can dispose of them because of the change in status. As handmaid, Hagar had been Sarah's property. Fourteen years later, not only is Hagar Abram's property, but Ishmael is Abram's son, not Sarah's. The text is explicit. "The matter distressed Abram greatly, for it concerned a son of his" (Gen. 21:11).

Why was Sarah so incensed? The term *(m)shq*, translated as "mocking," can refer to an act of impurity or idolatry. An act of impurity would be a more reasonable cause for rejection than simply "playing," as the term is usually translated.[31]

The confusion in this episode stems from verses 3 and 4 of this same Chapter 21. "Abram gave his newborn son, whom Sarah had borne him, the name Isaac. And when his son Isaac was eight days old, Abram circumcised him, as God commanded him." These dry statements of fact are from the hand of the *P* (priestly) strand, although the rest of the episode was written by redactor *E*. *P*'s contributions are belied by his constant preoccupation with purity of lineage; these verses are typical.

For instance, all the other women in Genesis, including the daughters of Lot, named their children. For the patriarch Abram, however, *P* saw fit to make a change. According to *P*, Abram not only names and circumcises Ishmael, he names and circumcises Isaac as well. It must be noted that most of the priestly contributions were not made until the fifth century B.C.E. In fact, the earliest law codes of Israel do not prescribe circumcision at all. Circumcision was practiced in antiquity by the Egyptians and most of the ancient Semitic peoples, but not

by the Sumerians, Babylonians, Assyrians, or Philistines. It was performed on males in childhood or puberty, rather than in infancy. Ishmael was circumcised at puberty — (by his Egyptian mother?). Hero-
dotus believed that Jews and others borrowed the practice from the
Egyptians [11:104]. But it is most unlikely that Isaac was exposed to
the ritual when he was eight days old.

The enigmatic term *(m)shq*, "mocking" used to describe Ishmael's
behavior, can also be rendered as something like "sexual fondling."[32]
Could it have had something to do with Isaac being uncircumcised? It
is very possible that Sarah did not circumcise Isaac, because she
seems to have held steadfastly to the traditions of her homeland, and
Babylonians did not practice circumcision. The Mesopotamian Sarah
may have abhorred this practice. When *P* felt the need to include a
notice of Isaac's circumcision at the beginning of the chapter, the story
lost its thrust.

The rite of circumcision could certainly have been a serious cause of
contention between Sarah and Abram. Abram, Mesopotamian himself, had not been circumcised until his son Ishmael was about thirteen years old. There would have been no conflict over the circumcision of Ishmael, since it was an ancient custom among the Egyptians.
Was Hagar the Egyptian introducing religio-cultural customs to
Abram which were unacceptable to Sarah?

The rite of circumcision is very significant in the account of the narratives because it is, above all, an act of initiation into a covenant community. The circumcision of Abram at age ninety-nine is symbolic of
the patriarch's initiation into a covenant with Elohim which he shared
with his son, Ishmael. What effect did this change have on Sarah? On
Ishmael? Was it circumcision rather than his change of status to slave
or son-of-a-slave that disqualified Ishmael as Sarah's heir?

It is interesting to note that Sarah herself did not conceive until after the circumcision of Abram and Ishmael and their initiation into the
new covenant. Their conversion meant that Sarah lost not only Ishmael as heir but also Abram as a husband who could have "built up"
her lineage with another woman (other than Hagar). Sarah's problem
was solved with the supernatural conception of Isaac. As it turned
out, however, the presence of an heir did not totally eliminate Sarah's
difficulty. She realized that she must rear her son Isaac away from the
influence the new covenant introduced into their community. In the
absence of law or central government, a ritual such as circumcision
could have been a way of gaining control.[33] Was the ritual being used
as a means of reducing Sarah's power?

There is certainly a great deal to be read between the lines in this story which culminates in Sarah's demand for the banishment of Hagar and Ishmael from Hebron. It seems that Sarah had serious reasons for her severity toward Hagar and her son. Eliminating a reasonable cause for the matriarch's decision points to only one conclusion: she had a jealous nature and a nasty temper. On this basis Speiser could comment: "[Ishmael's] 'playing' with Isaac need mean no more than that the elder boy was trying to amuse his little brother. There is nothing in the text to suggest that he was abusing him, a motive deduced by many troubled readers in their effort to account for Sarah's anger." And again, "Sarah's hatred of Hagar stemmed from the concubine's tactless behavior toward her childless mistress, and Abram was unwilling or unable to intervene in the bitter rivalry between the two women."[34] Actually Hagar had previously insulted Sarah, and the matriarch had punished her according to the law. In the "mocking" incident there was no rivalry because Sarah and Hagar had absolutely no interaction of any kind. What the text implies is that Hagar was bringing up her son Ishmael in a traditional Egyptian way, and this was not the influence Sarah wanted around Isaac. Differences in ideas about cultural education between two women hardly make them bitter enemies.

By stressing this point I hope to show how Sarah's character has been subtly distorted by Speiser's interpretation. If Ishmael was simply mocking or playing with Isaac, then Sarah's terrible show of anger, to the point where she has both Hagar and Abram's beloved son banished, becomes an uncontrollable fit of jealousy — a cruel and uncalled-for reaction.

This explanation is not only a calumny on Sarah's character; it also presents the patriarch as submissive and irresolute. By understanding the word *(m)shq* to refer to an important but undisclosed action with a religious aspect, we see Sarah's concern with circumcision as symbolic of the "idolatry" in Ishmael's influence on Isaac. Elohim's words to Abram corroborate this by admonishing him to heed his wife because the calling will come through her son. God also assures Abram that his son Ishmael will become a nation; and Abram obeys Sarah and sends Hagar and Ishmael away. We can well imagine Abram's emotional conflict as he expels his firstborn son. What authority did Sarah have to demand this act of her husband?

We must once more refer back to the old Babylonian laws, but this time to a code, almost two centuries earlier than that of Hammurapi, known as the Code of Lipit-Ishtar.[35] Section 25 reads as follows:

> If a man married a wife, and she bore him children and those children are living, and a *slave* also bore children *for her master*

40

(but) the father granted freedom to the slave and her children, the children of the slave shall not divide the estate with the children of their (former) master.

Dramatic and touching as the story is in the biblical text, with poor Hagar and her son being thrust out into the desert empty-handed, what Sarah actually demanded was something like, "Give that slave and her son their freedom so that Ishmael may not share in the inheritance with my son."

We know that Hagar and Ishmael got their freedom, since later the mother finds a wife for her son in her Egyptian homeland, a duty that would have belonged to Abram if they had remained his property, even if they no longer lived with him. That Ishmael continued to regard Abram as his father, even though Sarah did not permit him a share in the inheritance, is evident from the fact that after Abram's death Ishmael buried him in the cave of Machpelah.[36] According to sections 170–71 of the Code of Hammurapi, Abram could have acknowledged Ishmael as his son (but not as his heir) simply by stating the fact (possibly before witnesses). Abram willed all that he owned to Isaac. Though Abram gave gifts to his sons by Hagar and later wife Keturah while he was still living, they were excluded from the estate.

The parallels between the law of Lipit-Ishtar and the biblical text also reflect the change in the family situation: we are now being told of a slave and son(s) of the master, as compared to the previous episode, which dealt with a handmaid and the son of the mistress. The cause of this change will be discussed in chapter four.

Rebekah: Adversity in the Second Generation

Rebekah, married to Isaac, Sarah's son, is perhaps best remembered for the resourceful way in which she acquired Isaac's blessing for her younger son, Jacob (Gen. 27).

Rebekah had twins, Esau and Jacob. The firstborn was Esau, who, when he grew up, became a skillful hunter and was the favorite of his father. Jacob, by contrast, was a mild man, a shepherd, the favorite of his mother.

In this episode of Genesis, Isaac is old and blind. He feels that he may soon die, and asks for his firstborn to hunt some good game and make him a tasty dish so that he may give Esau the blessing. Rebekah overhears the exchange between Isaac and Esau and devises a way for Jacob to receive the blessing instead.

Rebekah cooks a tasty meal of game, dresses her younger son in his brother's clothes, and covers his hands and neck with kidskins so that he will smell and feel like his hairy brother. Then she sends Jacob to his father with the food. Isaac believes it is Esau and gives him the blessing. Shortly after, when Esau comes back, the scheme is discovered — but it is too late: the blessing once given cannot be taken back. Esau is furious. "First he took away my birthright [for a bowl of lentils] and now my blessing," he complains to his father (Gen. 25:29–34). This sequence was recorded by redactor J.

In the episode which follows the giving of the blessing, Rebekah is again concerned about the destiny of the younger Jacob. She says to Isaac, "I am disgusted with my life because of the Hittite women. If Jacob marries a Hittite woman like these [the wives of Esau], what good will my life be to me?" So Isaac sent for Jacob and blessed him and said, "You shall not take a wife from among the Canaanite women. Up, go to Paddam-Aram, to the house of Bethuel, your mother's father, and take a wife from among the daughters of Laban, your mother's brother." This passage was recorded by redactor P.

In J's story, Isaac is on his deathbed and Rebekah is distressed at his intention to bless the wrong son. In the next verse, however, Isaac seems to be full of life. He greets his son Jacob and seems in no way offended by the blessing incident. It is obvious that these two episodes are distinct and separate and do not follow a chronological sequence.

In J's version the author is trying to explain why Jacob instead of the firstborn Esau is to inherit the promise to Abram. His justification becomes Rebekah's conflict over the blessing, but he resolves it by depicting mother and son as crafty and deceitful, taking advantage of a blind old man.[37]

In P's story, Rebekah is distressed by different circumstances. Esau, following patriarchal custom, has brought his wives to the home of his parents, but the wives are local women, who observe local custom, and "were a source of bitterness for both Isaac and Rebekah."

Rebekah, it is clear, is intent on maintaining the traditions of her homeland. Jacob must marry according to matrifocal custom, where the man goes to live in the home of his wife's parents. He must also follow the rule of endogamy, marrying within the kinship group. Jacob is duly sent to find a wife at his mother's home in Mesopotamia.[38] He then lives for twenty years at the home of his mother's brother, Laban, in the area of Paddam-Aram. Following good patriarchal custom, commentators on this episode emphasize that, because of Rebekah, Jacob spent twenty years in exile![39]

We may note also that both J and P go to great lengths to show why the younger son becomes the successor, rather than the elder. Youngest daughters as well as sons were singled out for succession in the ancient Near East. There is a famous saga from Ugarit (Syria) in which the youngest daughter of King KRT is chosen by the semitic God Ba'al:[40] "To the youngest I shall give the birthright," he says.[41] Unfortunately, we cannot be sure whether the matriarchs of Genesis were also youngest daughters. Sarah and Rebekah had only brothers; we do not know the birth order of Milcah and her sister Iscah; and we know that Rachel was younger than her sister Leah, but not that she was the youngest child. Dinah, the daugher of Leah, had only brothers. Interestingly, Dinah's story ends after she was raped (Gen. 34), leaving only the twelve sons who became the famous tribes of Israel.

The Genesis narrative that most vividly indicates the matriarchs' partiality to ultimogeniture is perhaps the one dealing with the birthright of Rebekah's sons. Again, the interpretation of a passage is crucial to its meaning and impact.

According to the text, the twins conceived by Rebekah struggled in her womb, whereupon she enigmatically exclaimed: "If so, why do I exist?" The exact meaning of the Hebrew words of Rebekah's exclamation is difficult to ascertain. Speiser translates it most exactly,[42] I believe: "If this is how it is to be, why do I go on living?" Whatever the translation, the statement seems clearly to say that Rebekah is dissatisfied with her life. After twenty years of marriage, the matriarch is pregnant for the first time. What is the cause of her anxiety? Rebekah resolves to seek clarification from a divine source, and the oracle makes this announcement:

Two nations are in your womb,
Two peoples apart while still in your body;
One people shall be mightier than the other,
And the older shall serve the younger.

(Gen. 25:23)

In other words, the elder (Esau) would serve Jacob, the younger. The pronouncement given by the oracle must have satisfied Rebekah because the text does not mention the incident again. The firstborn of the twins was named Esau, and his brother, Jacob, according to the biblical text.

The text goes on to describe an incident between the brothers. "Once when Jacob was cooking a stew Esau came in from the open, famished." He asked Jacob to give him some stew and Jacob replied, "First, sell me your birthright." The famished Esau had no use for his birthright and sold it to Jacob. If Jacob's destiny had been sealed by the sacred oracle, why did he have to acquire the birthright from Esau for a bowl of lentils, and later deceive his old blind father? Did Isaac not know about the oracle?

43

There is a way of explaining this sequence that seems to make more sense. Let us assume that the social order observed by the matriarch Rebekah was not patriarchal and that succession by the youngest child[43] was customary to her. Isaac, however, was not as insistent as Rebekah on preserving the custom of ultimogeniture[44] (succession of the youngest); he had been brought up in patriarchal Canaan and was not averse to its male-oriented practice of primogeniture (succession of the eldest).

The struggle of the unborn children in her womb was a premonition of the worsening of the social difficulties which Rebekah had been experiencing in her environment. After all, she had been living in Canaan for twenty years. Filled with anxiety, she consulted the oracle who identified the struggle as a question of hierarchy: the older shall serve the younger. In other words, the destiny of the twins would be determined by the observance of ultimogeniture. Rebekah was satisfied because that is what she wanted. Nevertheless, someone in the family did not accept the fate decreed by the oracle. Since Esau gave up his birthright for a bowl of lentils, it must have been Isaac who "favored Esau" as a successor.

Certainly Isaac intended to give Esau the blessing rather than Jacob, despite the oracle and without Rebekah's knowledge. It was only when Rebekah overheard Isaac's intention that she devised a ruse to substitute the younger son. Furthermore, it is only after the blessing that Rebekah demanded that Jacob leave patriarchal Canaan altogether and find a wife for himself among her kin in Mesopotamia. Was the blessing a prerequisite for marriage with one of her brother's daughters?

The tremendous change underway, represented by the transfer of succession from the youngest to the eldest, is what caused Rebekah to question the very meaning of her existence: "If this is how it has to be, why do I go on living?" Even reaffirmation of her traditions by the oracle was ineffective: Esau, the eldest child, originally received the birthright, made exogamous marriages among the native women of Canaan, incorporated his wives into the household of his parents, and was singled out by his father for the blessing. This threat justifies the actions of Rebekah and Jacob. To maintain the old traditions Jacob retrieved his birthright from Esau, and Rebekah acquired the blessing for him from Isaac. Isaac, it seems, did not respect the pronouncement of the oracle any more than the customs of his wife's homeland. Instead, he conformed to the ways of Canaan, to the distress of his wife Rebekah, much as Abram before him had opposed his wife Sarah by circumcising himself and Ishmael.

We see, then, that the birthright[45] and the blessing, two different endowments, could be bestowed on either son — which implies that Rebekah's family at that time was not bound to one standard set of rules. This seems indicative of a period of transition, of a change in the social order involving this particular family.

Ironically, non-patriarchal Jacob became the patriarch of the Hebrews, instead of his truly patriarchal brother Esau.

Social Change and Rebekah's Lament

The blessing of Jacob had profound meaning and consequence for the life of Rebekah's son. Unlike the birthright, which was mainly concerned with the inheritance of property, the blessing was a transfer of spiritual succession. The core of the blessing gave Jacob abundance in grain and wine, but specifically for ritual purposes. The text may imply that Rebekah was intent on Jacob's inheriting spiritual or some form of priestly succession, whereas Jacob himself became predominantly concerned with the share of (material) inheritance.

Immediately after the blessing, and possibly because of it, we find Rebekah again directing the destiny of her youngest son. She must persuade Isaac to send Jacob to her homeland for a wife. Esau was already married, but his wives were not acceptable. Rebekah's distress over the changing family situation is masterfully described in two pertinent sentences: "I am disgusted with my life because of these Hittite women. If Jacob marries a Hittite woman like these from among the native women, what good will my life be to me?" The matriarch's lament was directed at the profound change in the social system which the "native women," wives of Esau, had introduced into her household. Rebekah wanted to make sure that her younger son married within her kinship group. She herself, her grandmother Milcah, and Sarah and her son Isaac all had endogamous marriages — they had all married within the extended family unit. Rebekah did not intend to break that custom.

Esau made a final effort to fit the mold. He "took to wife, in addition to the wives he had, Mahalath[46] the daughter of Ishmael, sister of Nebaioth." This in itself implies that the social customs of Ishmael (and therefore of his mother Hagar's people), were closer to Rebekah's than were those of the native women of Canaan.

Significantly, Rebekah's lament is rarely, if ever, analyzed by biblical commentators — probably because it is not understood. If Rebekah's lament is not included in the context of the struggle for social change, if it is narrowly visualized as the matriarch's personal aversion to the women of Canaan, it cannot make much sense. Once again it becomes clear that the matriarchs' story, the story of the women in Genesis, is not being told; it has been completely disregarded in favor of the story of the patriarchs.

Rebekah, like Sarah before her, was not a headstrong woman with a tendency to cruelty; she was exercising her authority — the matrilineal prerogative for the transmission of rights to offspring — while struggling to prevent patriarchal customs from encroaching on her life.

Rebekah is vividly depicted in Genesis. Despite the derogatory descriptions in the text, Rebekah's strength, beauty, and suffering have not been dimmed. The power of her personality is already evident when as a young girl she takes command of her destiny and leaves for Canaan. Her future appeared splendid; but reality proved otherwise. The descriptions of Rebekah's agony are very moving: "If so, why do I exist?" "I am disgusted with my life" and "What good will my life be to me?" We know nothing of the death of the matriarch Rebekah; but she was buried in the double cave, Machpelah, Sarah's grave (Gen. 49:31). Abram and Isaac, husbands of the matriarchs, were also buried there.

Rachel: Another Matriarch, Another Story

Jacob is sent to his mother's kin for a wife. Rebekah's brother Laban has two daughers, Leah and Rachel. Jacob eventually marries both of them.

The episode about Rachel describes how she too is forced to resort to unusual conduct so as to maintain her authority when threatened with social change (Gen. 31).

Laban, the sisters' father, is depicted in Genesis as a tyrannical and altogether unpleasant character where his daughters and son-in-law are concerned. After twenty years of subjection to Laban, Jacob and his wives plot to escape. "Jacob kept Laban the Aramean in the dark, not telling him that he was fleeing, and fled with all he had. Soon he was across the Euphrates and heading toward the hill country of Gilead." Laban "had gone to shear his sheep" and did not realize that the family had left until he was told about it three days later. Laban pursues Jacob and overtakes him in Gilead. "Why did you leave in secrecy and mislead me and not tell me?" Laban asks Jacob, telling him that had he known, he would have given them a festive send-off. But then he says to Jacob, "Very well, you had to leave because you were longing for your father's house; but why did you steal my gods?"

By "gods," Laban is referring to the *teraphim*, which Rachel had taken without Jacob's knowledge. The term *teraphim* is used on sever-

PLATE 6. Household dieties were used for the purpose of divination. These *teraphim* of Ishtar, shown one and one-half times actual size, are made of bone or ivory. *(Iraqi Museum, Baghdad. Courtesy State Organization for Antiquities.)*

PLATE 7. Teraphim were of various sizes, some as large as life. *(Left)* Terracotta statuette (actual size). Mesopotamian, Babylonian. Isin Larsa period, ca. 1900 B.C.E. *(The Metropolitan Museum of Art, Exhange, 1951, Oriental Institute, Chicago.)* *(Right)* Unglazed ceramic figure (three-quarters actual size). Mesopotamian, date unknown. *(The Metropolitan Museum of Art, Joint Expedition to Nippur, Rogers Fund, 1959).*

al occasions in the Bible. *The Encylopedia of Jewish Religion* describes *teraphim* as "Human images used as household gods for purposes of divination." Presumably these images were statuettes of various sizes (*see* Plates 6 and 7), small enough for Rachel to sit on or close to human size, such as the one kept in the home of David and Michal hundreds of years later. *Teraphim*, it seems, were a customary part of Israelite households until the Babylonian exile in the sixth century B.C.E.

Laban makes a seven-day journey to retrieve "his gods," as he puts it. Jacob, who is quite innocent of their disappearance, allows Laban to search for them, saying: "I was frightened at the thought that you would take your daughters from me by force. But anyone with whom you find your gods shall not remain alive!" Jacob is unaware that Rachel has them. The enraged father goes first to the tent of his daughter Leah and then to the tent of Rachel. As he enters her tent, Rachel is sitting on a camel cushion in which she had hidden the statuettes. Laban rummages through her tent, and Rachel says to him "Let not my lord take it amiss that I cannot rise before you, for the period of women is upon me." Laban, of course, leaves without having found his household gods.

What is the reason for Rachel's seemingly deceitful act of stealing her father's *teraphim?* Rachel, like her predecessors Sarah and Rebekah, is presented by the redactors as cunning and scheming; and like Sarah's banishing of Hagar and the deception of Isaac by Rebekah, Rachel's deceit has no apparent justification. Without a rational explanation for her behavior, we are left with the uneasy feeling that the matriarch's character lacks integrity.

Commentators have proposed a variety of assumptions on the theme of the stolen images. Speiser[47] assumes that Jacob was Laban's heir but that Rachel, knowing her father's greed, did not believe that Laban would honor her husband's right to inherit the *teraphim*, so he suggests she stole them. The *teraphim*, Speiser surmises, symbolized title to property rights. A. E. Draffkorn,[48] while agreeing that the *teraphim* symbolized title to property, goes a little further by suggesting that daughters too had inheritance rights, and that Rachel was therefore safeguarding her own interests. Another commentator, M. Greenberg,[49] argues that Rachel wanted the protection of the gods on her journey and that the secrecy of the decision of Jacob and his wives to flee Laban made the theft necessary. Thompson[50] does not agree that possession of the statues had any legal significance, but considers them to be more of a family heirloom. Rachel, he asserts, "has stolen the gods because, as gods, they are valuable to her." Thompson does in fact make a good point against the position (of Speiser for instance) that Jacob was Laban's heir.[51] Who then is Laban's heir? I think this question must be answered before we can attempt to understand the *teraphim* incident.

Before the departure, Jacob had Rachel and Leah called to the field, where his flock was, to discuss with them their father Laban's unjust conduct toward him. "I see your father's manner toward me is not as it has been in the past; but the God of my father has been with me. As you know, I have served your father with all my might; but your father has cheated me, changing my wages time and again." In a dream, an angel has told him to "leave this land and return to the land of your birth." The fact that Jacob consults with his wives gives weight to their reply: "Have we still a share in the inheritance of our father's house? Are we not reckoned by him as outsiders? For he sold us and then used up our purchase price. Truly, all the wealth that God has taken away from our father belongs to us and our children. Now then, do just as God has told you."

The case of Rachel and Leah is an interesting one. They were entitled to a share in Laban's property and also a portion of their own dowries for their children. According to Old Babylonian law, both the womens' inheritance (*zittu*) and their part of their dowries would pass to their children.[52] The *terhatu* ("bride price") Jacob had paid for his wives was seven years' labor for each woman. Laban had exacted a *terhatu* for both his daughters from Jacob; but Laban had not given the daughters the portion of bridewealth which belonged to their children. This had already incensed the sisters. How were they to trust their father with the inheritance? All the wealth that Jacob was able to reclaim was rightfully theirs, as both bridewealth and inheritance.

Apart from the inheritance, there was a question of birthright. Who was head of household? The women mentioned themselves and their children as Laban's heirs, so evidently Jacob had no claim to the estate. Nor was Jacob in a patriarchal position of authority vis-à-vis his wives or his father-in-law. With Jacob out of the picture we are left with Laban and his two daughters as possible head of the family. We know that the sisters claim a portion of the bridewealth and a share in the estate of their father. But what about ownership of the *teraphim*, the sacred statuary?

We can start with an almost minute clue, a question of hierarchy. Rachel, the younger, is always mentioned before her sister: Rachel and Leah, not Leah and Rachel. The order of names was significant in ancient times. Rachel is the youngest daughter (Laban also had sons); her name is placed before that of her elder sister; she and not Leah takes the images. Among some peoples where descent is traced through the youngest daughter, it is she who is responsible for the religious obligations within the family.[53] Did Rachel hold such a position in the family, and did she consider that she had a right to the sacred images? Rachel's position will be explored in greater depth in chapter four, but we may note here that the conflict of the sisters with their father is similar to that of Sarah and Rebekah with their respective husbands. The women seem to have ideas about social customs very different from those of their menfolk.

Another hint of Rachel's special position in the family comes in the sequence in which Rachel, childless after many years of marriage, says to Jacob almost the exact words used by Sarah before her: "Here is my maid Bilhah. Consort with her, that she may bear on my knees and that through her, my house too will be built up." Rachel's situation illustrates more specifically than Sarah's that the matriarch's intention was to build up her own house or lineage and that she was not concerned with whether her husband had issue. Jacob already had four sons by Leah; Rachel, then, was anxious about having her own heir, not Jacob's. Rachel was observing the same rule in the Code of Hammurapi that Sarah had followed. And those rules applied only to women of a certain religious rank in Babylonia.

Rachel's use of this rule and her carrying off of the *teraphim* both possess a religious aspect. Rachel had every right to the symbols of her position (if that is what the sacred objects represented to her), especially after the behavior of her father toward herself, her sister, and her husband. She understood perfectly the importance of her act and wisely decided to keep it secret even from her husband. Because possession of sacred images betokened clan leadership and spiritual power, Rachel could act without peril to her husband and ensure succession to her own offspring.

However, once in Canaan, Jacob told his household, "Rid yourselves of the alien gods in your midst." Rachel's statuary must have come to light just before her death if they had not been found before that. Perhaps because of the *teraphim* and the power they had represented to Rachel, Jacob took two of her grandchildren, sons of her house, adopted them as his own, and blessed the youngest, Ephraim, over Manasseh, the eldest, as the matriarch's custom prescribed: the younger would inherit over the elder.

The patriarchs acquiesced to their wives' Mesopotamian laws, traditions, and customs even though these did not always agree with their own increasingly patriarchal ideals. It took many generations before the matriarchs' traditions were completely overruled.[54]

IV

EXAMINING THE NON-PATRIARCHAL SOCIAL SYSTEM AND GENEALOGY IN GENESIS

Our examination of the social aspects of life as described or implied in the Genesis narratives showed that they do not fit the traditional concept of a patriarchal society. We found that the matriarchs fought for and defended customs that prevailed in their homeland in Mesopotamia, while the patriarchs followed those customs only when their wives insisted on it. Abram accepted Sarah's banishment of his first-born, Ishmael; Isaac agreed to Rebekah's urging to send Jacob to his mother's brother's house for a wife. In both cases the women were exercising a social right or obligation, a right accepted and acknowledged by their husbands. The matriarchs would not change their traditions for the more patriarchal system surrounding them in Canaan.

This is not an attempt to establish a connection between the matriarchs and the so-called matriarchate. I am not familiar with the enormous variety of social systems that exist and have existed in the past, and do not mean to identify the society of Genesis with any one particular social system. The aim here is simply to show that many of the customs observed by the matriarchs did not conform to some of the basic precepts of patriarchy (such as primogeniture), and that the matriarchs' practices were abolished only slowly.

It is important to remember that the Genesis narratives were written down after a long period of oral tradition, during which each segment was changed or embellished according to the inclinations of the teller. The accounts were recorded by more than one scribe or redactor, and finally the various sources were fused together into what is now our biblical text. Because of this, many elements indispensable to the reconstruction of the matriarchs' social system have been lost.

In this chapter we will examine some of the features in the Genesis narratives that are not typical of a patriarchal system. These elements, listed below, cannot be said to constitute a matriarchal system either; for this reason it is preferable to refer to the social system in the narratives as *non-patriarchal*.

1. Matrilineal descent
2. Endogamy (marriage within the descent group)
3. Ultimogeniture (succession by the youngest child)
4. Matrilocal residence
5. Sororal polygyny

Matrilineal Descent

Matrilineal descent, descent through the female line, is the norm in the narratives. But what happened if a woman had no daughters, as in Sarah's case? Did Milcah belong to Sarah's blood line via her father, Sarah's uterine brother Harran? Or was Harran's wife related to Sarah? Without knowledge of the kinship relations between Harran's wife and Sarah, or Sarah's mother, it is impossible to reconstruct a kinship or marriage system in Sarah's descent group. Because of the considerable evidence in the texts that Sarah's mother's descendants followed a non-patriarchal social system, I do not believe that they were committed to patriliny, as *P's* lists of "begettings" indicate.

According to the narratives, birth and marriage followed strict regulations. A woman's children were members of her descent group (and therefore her mother's), and remained so provided they married within that descent group. However, only uterine siblings — that is, children of the same mother — were recognized as members of the same family group.[55] Nonuterine siblings, children who had the same father but different mothers, were not members of the same family unit but might belong to the same descent group via their mother.

The relationship of Sarah and Abram is one that would be found in a system of matriliny. It is clearly stated in Genesis that they had the same father *but different mothers* and that they were married. Their union is not regarded as incestuous. Terah was the father of both Sarah and Abram; but because we have no record of who their mothers were, it is difficult to tell whether they were members of the same descent group.

Pharaoh's angry question, "Why did you say, 'She is my sister'?" and Abimelech's plea to God, "He himself said to me, 'She is my sister,'" are clear indications that the kings understood Sarah to be Abram's *uterine* sister. Abram's definition of siblings was not that of the kings. When Abram pleads with Sarah to say that he is her brother rather than her husband, it is on the assumption that the kings will take them to be uterine siblings, children of the same mother. Since children of the same mother could not be husband and wife, Abram implied that Sarah was not married to him.

The important question of whether Ishmael was regarded as Sarah's or Abram's offspring can be further clarified. Initially, Ishmael represented a son of the body for Sarah, a member of her descent group; but after the birth of Isaac, a true son of the body, Sarah was able to reject Ishmael on the grounds that he was not truly her flesh and blood and therefore could not "share in the inheritance" with her son Isaac. The inheritance, of course, did go to Isaac and not to Ishmael. Ishmael is mentioned with Isaac as burying their father, an indication that he was regarded as a son of Abram, even though he did not inherit.[56]

Of Harran's descendants, we find Milcah and her sons are accepted into Sarah's descent group but not Lot, his only son, who in patriliny would have played a significant role in the narrative. Instead, we find that the progeny of Lot's daughters (Lot's descendants) are specifically excluded from "the congregation of the Lord." Speiser suggests[57] that since Lot and his daughters believed that they were the only people left on earth after the destruction of Sodom, the daughters should be praised rather than condemned for their incest, which was occasioned only by their wish to perpetuate their father's seed. But this explanation is quite invalid. The commentator overlooks an important sentence in the text which tells us that from Sodom, Lot and his daughters fled first to Zoar and then to the hill country (Gen. 19:20-32). They could not possibly have thought they were the only people on earth if they had just left the town of Zoar. The sexual relationship of Lot with his daughters raises the same question of incest as that raised by the relationship of Sarah and Abram. But it too can be explained. Although both are examples of a type of relationship later condemned by patriarchal law (Lev. 18:6-16), in a matrilineal society the implications are not the same. From a matrilineal perspective neither Lot nor Abram was considered to be a blood relative of the women he had intercourse with. Even though Lot's daughters may have recognized him as their biological parent, they were heirs of their mother (see Table 2).

Unfortunately, we again have no information as to the origin of the daughters' mother, the wife of Lot. She most probably was not from Mesopotamia, since she was not mentioned in the migration. We hear of her only when the destruction of Sodom was imminent, and then not even by name. It was she who, defying the order not to look back

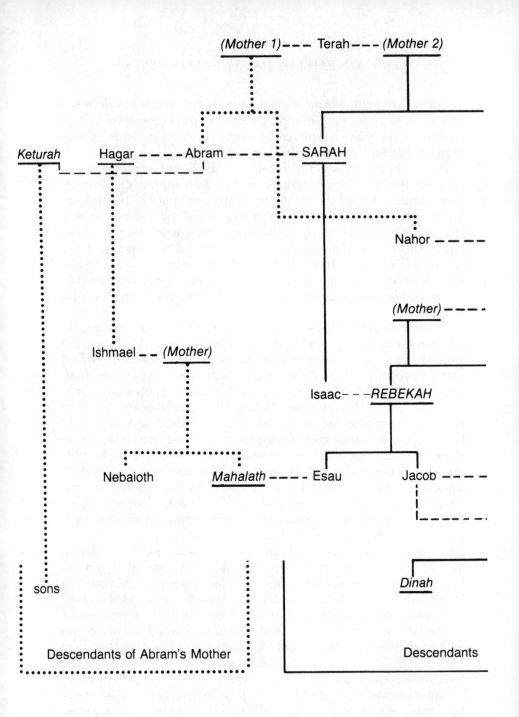

Table 2. Genealogy

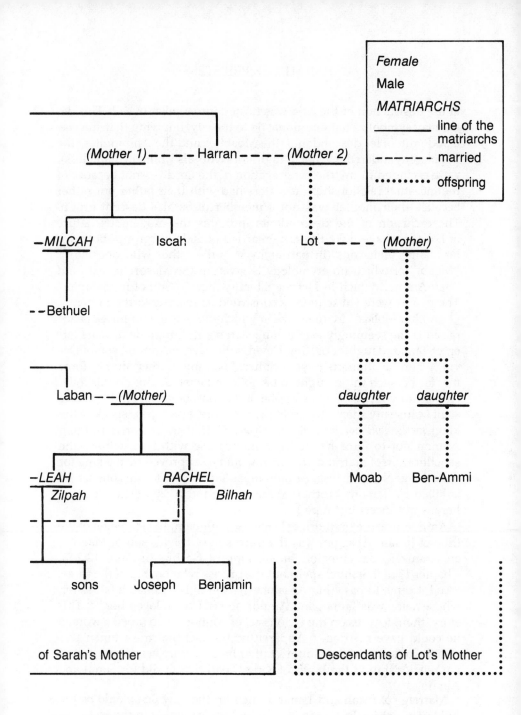

Female

Male

MATRIARCHS

———— line of the matriarchs

– – – – – married

·········· offspring

(Mother 1) – – – – Harran – – – – (Mother 2)

–MILCAH   Iscah

– –Bethuel

Lot – – – – *(Mother)*

Laban – – *(Mother)*

–LEAH   *RACHEL*
Zilpah   *Bilhah*

sons   Joseph   Benjamin

of Sarah's Mother

daughter   daughter

Moab   Ben-Ammi

Descendants of Lot's Mother

According to the Mothers

at the destruction of the city, was turned into a pillar of salt. This detail may symbolize her emotional tie to the city, implying that she was a Sodomite. Her descendants, the Moabites and the Ammonites, the people engendered by her daughters (who also remain nameless), were excluded from "the congregation of the Lord" — not because of the incestual relationship the sisters had with their father but rather because their mother was not a member of Sarah's descent group. The exclusion of the descendants indicates the exogamous nature of Lot's marriage. Like Esau, he married outside his group. Both sisters name their sons (in patriarchy it is the father who does so):[58] "Moab," of which no etymology is given in the Masoretic text, and "Ben-Ammi," which in Hebrew literally means "son of my people." The names were subsequently construed as relating to the father.[59]

Another biblical circumstance in which the question of incest is not raised is the seemingly astonishing statement, hundreds of years later, of Tamar, daughter of King David, who says to Amnon, son of David, when he attempts to seduce her: "No, my brother, do not force me; for no such thing ought to be done in Israel: do not do this folly. And as for you, you will be as one of the fools of Israel. And I, where shall I cause my shame to go? Now, therefore, I pray you, speak to the king; *for he will not hold me from you.*"[60] That is, Tamar is begging Amnon not to force her to have intercourse with him without the sanctification of matrimony, which would be approved by the king for the asking. Nevertheless, Amnon rapes Tamar, and for this offense he is killed by Tamar's brother Absalom (II Sam. 13:29). (The violation here is not incest but rape.)

Amnon was the firstborn of David by Ahinoam, the Jezreelite of the tribe of Judah. Absalom was the third son of David, son of Maacah, an Aramean, daughter of Talmai, king of Geshur (II Sam. 12:2-3). Chapter 13 of II Samuel spells out the precise relationship of the three: "And it came to pass that Absalom the son of David had a fair sister, whose name was Tamar; and Amnon son of David, loved her."[61] This story, then, focuses on the vicious act of Amnon, who raped a woman he could have married.[62] Apparently, the fact that the woman was also the offspring of her suitor's father had no more bearing on a marital relationship in the times of King David than it did for Sarah and Abram.

Marriage of Sarah and Tamar to their brothers, which would be forbidden in patriarchy, is mentioned without comment in the texts, implying that the marriage of non-uterine siblings was acceptable to the redactors. It is possible that the non-uterine sister–brother union of Sarah and Abram was the precedent for marriage between non-uterine siblings in Israelite royalty, as suggested in the Tamar–Amnon story.

Endogamy: Descent Group Requirements in Genesis

Provided the bloodline was reckoned through the mother, a woman could legitimately marry a man who was the son of her father but whose mother was a woman *other* than her own mother. Kinship was acknowledged only when group members could claim to belong to the same mother's bloodline. This descent group requirement in Genesis explains why Milcah was a member of Sarah's descent group whereas Lot was not (*see* Table 2).

One way of deciphering the descent lines in Genesis is to separate the accounts of the different redactors. In Lot's case, for instance, there is a difference between authors *J* and *P*. It is *P* who tells us that Lot was the son of Harran (Gen. 11:27, 31, and 12:5). The older version written by *J* simply records that "Abram went as YHWH told him, and Lot went with him" (Gen. 12:4). But when *J* recounts the genealogy of Harran, he does it this way: "Harran died in the lifetime of his father Terah, in his native land, in Ur of the Chaldeans. Abram and Nahor took wives; the name of Abram's wife was Sarai, and Nahor's wife was Milcah, daughter of Harran, *the father of Milcah and Iscah*" (Gen. 11:28-29). Nowhere does *J* mention Lot as a descendant of Harran.

In this light, it can be conjectured that Milcah's mother belonged to a descent group different from Lot's mother. In other words Harran, like his father Terah, had two wives: one the mother of Milcah and Iscah and the other the mother of Lot, the former being an accepted member of Sarah's descent group. Because of this, Milcah's son Bethuel and his daughter Rebekah were also acknowledged members of the group, whereas Lot and his progeny were not. In non-patriarchal terms, Lot was a member of his mother's group and his daughters were related to his wife, their mother; therefore, no incest occurred. Traditionally, the names of Moab and Ben-Ammi are shown to relate to the father, emphasizing a patriarchal order but at the same time making incestuous the relationship between father and daughters. In the narrative an effort is made to condone Lot because he was drunk.[63]

Isaac did marry within his descent group but one of his sons did not: Esau, we are told, distressed his parents because he married "native women." Thus his descendants, the Edomites, were not members of his mother's descent group. Jacob, upon the insistence of his mother Rebekah, did marry into her family, and his descendants thus became members of his mother's descent group.

SARAH THE PRIESTESS

Ultimogeniture

A feature of patrilineal descent is primogeniture: the firstborn male inherits his father's authority and a major portion of his father's estate. But ultimogeniture, succession by the youngest, is the norm in Genesis: Isaac, the son of Abram, is chosen instead of the firstborn Ishmael; Bethuel, the son of Nahor, is chosen instead of Milcah's firstborn, Uz; Jacob, the son of Isaac, is chosen instead of Rebekah's firstborn, Esau. Of Jacob's descendants, Leah's youngest (according to J), Judah, became more prominent than the oldest, Reuben; and Rachel's youngest, Benjamin, became more prominent than his elder brother Joseph, in that it was Saul, a descendant of Benjamin, who was annointed first king of Israel. The line of Judah, of course, boasts a dynasty of kings, beginning with David and his son Solomon, both youngest sons of their mothers. Finally, Ephraim, son of Joseph (son of Rachel), was chosen over his elder brother Manasseh to receive Jacob's blessing. Neither Isaac, Bethuel, Jacob, Judah, nor Benjamin was a firstborn son.

As for the women in Genesis it is almost impossible to tell the order of their birth because the text gives us such sparse information about them. Of Harran's descendants, Milcah and her sister Iscah are recorded by J, but Lot is not mentioned with them. The inclusion of Iscah must have had some significance that either J or his source chose not to elucidate. Nevertheless a strong tradition must have barred the redactors from omitting Iscah's name, a tradition, presumably, in which a sister had an important function; this tradition is apparent also in Genesis 4:22, in which Naamah,[64] sister of Tubal-Cain, is mentioned only by name. It can be surmised that Naamah and Iscah were originally recorded to categorize the descent group (or other characteristic) of their siblings Tubal-Cain and Milcah. In non-patriarchal terms, Naamah and Tubal-Cain were uterine siblings, as were Milcah and Iscah. It is also possible that Milcah is named before her sister Iscah because she was younger, just as Rachel is named before Leah. Among Harran's descendants, the sequence of Lot's birth is not significant and is not mentioned in the genealogy of J because he was not the uterine sibling of Milcah and Iscah, did not belong to the same descent group as they, and was therefore not considered by Sarah or Abram as heir.

Matrilocal Residence

Many matrilineal societies require that a man leave the locality of his birth at marriage and go to live with the relatives of his wife. This type of residence, called matrilocal, keeps a core of related females (grandmothers, mothers, sisters, daughters, granddaughters) together in one locality, along with their imported husbands.[65] The three generations of Genesis matriarchs — Sarah, Rebekah, and Leah/Rachel — were all involved with matrilocal residence.

When we first meet them, the matriarch Sarah and her husband Abram are living in Ur of the Chaldeans, Sarah's birthplace. Abram the northerner went to live with his wife in the south. Genesis does not record anything about Sarah's mother, Milcah's mother, or the reason for Terah's migration to Haran from Ur, so it is impossible to confirm matrilocal residence for them.

Rebekah's case is a complex one: she lived with her mother and brother and was expected to have a matrilocal marriage, and yet she chose otherwise. However, before reviewing Rebekah's story it is important to look at her family background, because this particular family gives us great insight into the social climate of these matrilineal kinship groups.

The most enigmatic of all the characters in the narratives is that of Bethuel.[66] Who in fact was Bethuel? The descendants of Milcah and Nahor are listed by J (Gen. 22:21-22) from the firstborn Uz to Jidlaph, "and Bethuel, Bethuel being the father of Rebekah." In the long account of Rebekah's betrothal (67 verses), Bethuel is mentioned three times as Rebekah's father. Only once does he appear in the narrative itself: "Laban and Bethuel answered." Even here, Bethuel's son Laban is mentioned before him. Because of this, most scholars regard the sentence as intrusive material. If, as scholars agree, Genesis 22:22a-23 and 24:50 are interpolations and Bethuel did not exist, who was Rebekah's father? Simpson suggests that Bethuel is a substitution for Laban,[67] meaning presumably that Laban was Rebekah's father rather than her brother. This seems untenable since there would be no reason for changing the relationship expressly stated in the text: "Now Rebekah had a brother whose name was Laban" (Gen. 24:29). Furthermore, in the sequel to the story, Rebekah's son Jacob would have been sent to marry his mother's sisters, Leah and Rachel, which would complicate the relationships unnecessarily.

Bethuel is represented as being alive but virtually without authority. His inconsequential position is particularly apparent because Rebekah's mother plays such a prominent part in her daughter's betrothal.[68] Rebekah's mother is mentioned three times directly (Gen. 24:28, 53, 55), and twice indirectly (57, 58). After meeting Abram's emissary, Rebekah runs to her mother's house to tell her mother and brother what transpired; the emissary gives presents to Rebekah's mother as well as to her brother; and both Laban and his mother request that the girl remain with them a few days longer.

The name of Rebekah's mother, like the names of all the matriarchs' mothers (in keeping with patriarchal tradition), has been edited out. I believe, however, that the name of Rebekah's father, Bethuel, was originally the name of Rebekah's mother,[69] and that the change of the name from feminine to masculine was a redactor's clumsy attempt to introduce a father figure into Rebekah's matrifocal community. Since the whole narrative of Rebekah's betrothal centers around her mother, her brother, and her mother's household, when we read in verse 50 that "Laban and Bethuel answered," it seems reasonable to infer that, later in the same paragraph, the words, "But her brother and her mother said," refer to the same persons in the same order. This would also eliminate the problem of why Laban is named before his father.

As the biblical text now stands, Rebekah's brother Laban greets the emissary of Abram, takes him to the house, offers food and drink, and hears his story. It is Laban and his mother who receive presents and negotiate the marriage. Speiser concludes from this that there is "little doubt that Bethuel was no longer alive at the time."[70]

This prominence of a mother and brother in the marriage arrangements of a girl, and in receiving a guest, is similar to the customs found by Chie Nakane among the Khasi of India. In a chapter entitled "Marriage with an Heiress," Nakane says: "The family system is clearly reflected in their daily behavior. When we visited the household of a youngest daughter, if a man (obviously the husband) came first to greet us, he would always say, 'Please wait, my wife (or mother-in-law) is coming.' And it was the wife who entertained us, offering tea or pan and discussing matters with us, while her husband remained silent in a corner of the room, or in the next room. If her uncle or brother was there, he would be the person who talked to us."[71] Rebekah's father may have been silent rather than dead.

Finally, the question of Bethuel would be resolved in a matrilineal society like the one we are discussing if Milcah had a daughter rather than a son. Just before Sarah's death, "word reached Abraham" that "Milcah too has borne children" (Gen. 22:20), with Bethuel mentioned as the last child. "Milcah too," according to Speiser (p. 167), refers to Gen. 21:1-2 where the birth of Isaac is recorded. Since Isaac is destined to be the husband of Bethuel's daughter, this notice, arriving as it did before the death of Sarah, seems to imply that the matriarch's son has been assured of a wife in Milcah's direct matri-line.

Why is the account of Rebekah's betrothal told in such detail if, in effect, it belies a non-patriarchal setting? The story of Rebekah's betrothal portrays a significant change in this community: from matrilocal to patrilocal residence. Why did Rebekah make a patrilocal marriage? That Isaac did not go to live with his bride's family was obviously an exception to the rule. Abram, for whatever reason, was adamantly opposed to his son's returning to Mesopotamia. "On no account are you to take my son back there," Abram admonishes his emissary, who is under oath. "What if the woman does not consent to follow me?" the envoy asks. "If she does not consent to follow you, you shall be clear of my oath; but do not take my son back there" (Gen. 24:4-8). Abram repeats his injunction twice. It is quite clear that both Abram and his emissary are aware of the custom: Isaac should have gone to Mesopotamia.

Laban and his mother allow Rebekah to make a patrilocal marriage, but seemingly with some misgivings. When the envoy is eager to leave immediately, mother and son request that the girl remain with them ten days longer, but the emissary insists on leaving without delay. Rebekah is called upon to make the final decision: "Will you go with this man?" And Rebekah says, "I will."

Rebekah goes to Isaac in Canaan. After meeting her, Isaac "brought her into the tent of his mother Sarah, and he took Rebekah as his wife." Although Rebekah makes a patrilocal marriage, Isaac provides a semblance of matrilocality by consummating his marriage to Rebekah in the tent of his mother, Sarah.[72]

Later Jewish legend has it that a cloud, which had been visible over Sarah's tent and then vanished at her death, reappeared when Rebekah entered the tent.[73] In other words, the union was blessed, and Sarah's spiritual heritage would be continued through Rebekah.

Sororal Polygyny in the Narratives

According to Kathleen Gough, sororal polygyny (sisters marrying the same man) is fostered in matrilineal systems that are matrilocal and have a weak descent group. In the absence of a large, strongly structured, and stably located descent group, sororal polygyny is advantageous to women because it increases a husband's commitment to this conjugal unit and to his children.[74]

The only example of sororal polygyny in Genesis is that of the sisters Leah and Rachel marrying the same man, Jacob. Later, Leviticus (18:18) expressly forbids sororal polygyny even though the practice continued in Israel. Genesis 29 is in effect concerned with which of the two sisters should marry first, and not with whether they should marry the same man. Jacob's marriage was, of course, matrilocal, since he went to the region of Haran to live with his wives. Laban's greeting, "You are truly my bone and flesh," as these terms are explained by Claude Levi-Strauss,[75] is definitely a non-patriarchal statement.

Matrilocal residence and their own close ties to matri-kin[76] gave Rachel and Leah extensive participation in decision making: they decided between themselves whom Jacob would service as sexual partner; they named their own offspring; they made decisions on the distribution of family wealth; they gave Jacob their approval when he decided to flee from Laban their father and to return to Canaan; and Rachel took the *teraphim,* the family religious symbols, on her own authority, against her father's wishes and without even the knowledge of her husband.[77]

Once in Canaan, however, Jacob slowly appropriated the authority of his sororal wives. He buried the *teraphim* and established his family in the new land. It is possible that Jacob, like Abram before him, was not circumcised until he was initiated into the same covenant as Abram and Isaac, symbolized by his change of name to Israel.

Shortly after that Rachel died, giving birth to a son she named Ben-Oni, "son of my sorrow." Here, too, Jacob assumed her prerogative by renaming this son Benjamin "son of the right hand."

Rachel's grave, like that of Sarah, is recorded in Genesis (35:19, 48:7); Jacob erected a pillar to mark her tomb. The site was still mentioned as being in existence in the fourth century C.E., indicating that it was highly regarded and revered for many centuries. Rachel's traditional tomb is one built by the Crusaders in the twelfth century on the road to Bethlehem, rather than its true location, which was in Ephratha in the territory of Benjamin. This is due to an error in the Book of Ruth (4:11).

In the economic sphere, the expectations of Rachel and Leah were non-patriarchal. They demanded their inheritance, which they considered to belong to them and to their children, not to their husband or father. It was supposedly not until the time of Moses that daughters were allowed to inherit, and then only if there were no sons in the family. According to the biblical text, Laban had sons as well as daughters (Gen. 30:35 and 31:1).

Sororal polygyny was not a great conflict for Rachel and Leah, as commentators have led us to believe. Their dissent has been stressed more than their concurrence.

Growth of Patriarchal Influence

Persistence in the texts of such non-patriarchal features as ultimogeniture, matrifocality, choice of a successor, and sororal polygyny, together with matrilocality and matrilineality (which can sometimes form part of a patriarchal structure), show the authority and respect demanded by women in early biblical times. Because of the stature of the matriarchs, it is important to notice certain omissions which (along with the repression of other elements) indicate the authors' suppression of women in the narratives. Perhaps the most striking example is that the names of the women's mothers have been omitted:

Sarah's mother (Terah's wife) — no name
Milcah's mother (Harran's wife) — no name
Rebekah's mother (Bethuel's wife) — no name
Rachel and Leah's mother (Laban's wife) — no name

The lack of this information, coupled with the change of residence from Mesopotamia to Canaan, makes it all but impossible to trace a full kinship system in these narratives (*see* Table 2). Mothers nevertheless held acknowledged responsible positions in ancient times. Where marriage is polygynous a mother's role in the bringing up of her own children and her interest in preserving her own lineage are emphasized.

Some omissions in Genesis are indirect; but sometimes they occur only in translation, not in the original text.

The Hebrew term *akara* can mean "barren" or "childless," but is always translated "barren" in the English text. Sarah, Rebekah, and Rachel are all portrayed in these translations as physically incapable of giving birth to children. "Barrenness" implies that the women were able to conceive only with the help of divine intervention. "Childlessness" would suggest that the matriarchs had a choice to be without child. The biblical matriarchs did have a choice; they were not barren.

Genesis does not make it clear that succession of the youngest child was also a choice of the matriarch. The four women opted to preserve the customs of their matrifocal tradition even after they had moved to Canaan.

In biblical times, marriage was a public act of status affirmation, which very often conferred prestige on either or both of the contracting partners. However, Genesis describes many kinds of unions, of which marriage is only one. We also find non-legal unions such as those of the patriarchs and their second wives or concubines; religiously sanctioned unions like those of Sarah and Rebekah with the kings; and unorthodox unions such as those of Sarah and Abram, or Lot and his daughters. In each case it was the woman who chose her sexual partner or the partner of her husband or son. Sarah, Rachel, and Leah gave their handmaids to their husbands of their own free will. Rebekah chose to marry Isaac after her mother and brother consented to the betrothal, and later sent her own son Jacob to find a wife in her mother's community. I strongly suspect that Rebekah and Rachel's unions were predetermined by their parents, particularly because both women were priestesses, although the final decision was theirs to make.

It is important to attempt to recreate an image of the society the matriarchs were struggling to maintain because it may give us an insight into the imbalance between men and women created by patriarchy. This approach may be helpful in clarifying many of the enigmatic passages encountered in Genesis. Matrilineality, matrilocality, and a specific non-patriarchal structure play an unquestionable part in these narratives and genealogies. Nonetheless, progressive patriarchal influence is clearly evident.

Matrilineal descent and endogamy (marriage within the descent group or tribe) were strictly observed by the matriarchs, though not necessarily by the patriarchs. Ishmael, the offspring of one of Abram's exogamous unions, was central to the changing social order as experienced by Sarah. Being of Egyptian descent, he was circumcised at puberty. Simultaneous with Ishmael's rite of passage was the circumcision of his father, Abram, in honor of a covenant recently made with his God. The covenant involved a promise on the part of the deity: "I give this land you sojourn in to you and your offspring to come, all the land of Canaan, as an everlasting possession; I will be their God." In other words, the practice of circumcision would allow the transfer of title patrilineally through the generations indefinitely. The covenant demanding circumcision is, according to the text, linked to the inheritance of the land of Canaan, to patriliny, and to the God Elohim. This tremendous change in the social order of Sarah's family had far-reaching consequences for the next three generations. But Sarah herself exercised considerable authority over her own life and the destiny of her sons and handmaid.

In the second generation, Rebekah was under the supervision of her mother and brother while she was still a young girl, but her father played no authoritative part within the family. Rebekah came to Mamre and took Sarah's place after the matriarch's death. She strongly expressed her displeasure at the change in the social structure of *her* family twenty years later. Genesis gives us an insight into the traumatic experience of Rebekah's struggle to maintain what in her view was the rightful precedence of her younger son. Her concern with the perpetuation of the descent line was the focus of dissent between herself and her husband. In this respect, the effort exerted by her husband was ineffective.

Abram and Isaac are both depicted as passively acknowledging the influence of their wives. Jacob, on the other hand, was cunning rather than passive. His dispute was not with his wives; it was with Laban, his father-in-law. Rachel and Leah agreed with their husband that their father had treated him abominably, and they determined to go to Canaan with him, leaving their patriarchally inclined father.

The disagreements between Jacob and Laban were connected with possessions and material wealth; the conflicts of Leah, and particularly Rachel (whose experiences are similar to Sarah's), centered primarily on their need for descendants. It is also significant that it was Rachel who took the *teraphim*. Rachel, not Leah, is the protagonist of the story, not simply (as tradition implies) because she was the beloved of Jacob, but because she had an important function to accomplish.[78] Rachel's function, like that of her predecessors Sarah and Rebekah, was concerned in part with group membership; one of the characteristics of the matriarchs' kinship group was ultimogeniture. It is certainly significant that the three matriarchs were concerned with providing themselves with heirs, irrespective of those their husbands might have preferred or recognized.

According to David Bakan, "The issue of matrilineality versus patrilineality is important only where there is exogamy; under endogamy the issue simply does not arise. For if marriages take place only within the group, the lineages of the male and the female are in common, and a position on whether identity goes through the female or the male is not required."[79] That is, it makes little difference whether one traces descent through the female or male line if marriages occur within an extended family group. In the traditional genealogical table of the patriarchs (*see* Appendix B), descent is both patrilineal and endogamous. This table, however, poses a problem: it does not explain why Lot, the nephew of Abram, was not considered Abram's heir before he had issue of his own. In Genesis 15:3 Abram says to God, "Since you have granted me no offspring, one of my household will be my heir." Lot did not qualify as Abram's heir because he did not belong to the descent group of Abram's mother. He did not qualify as Sarah's heir either because he was not a member of her descent group. Lot's descendants were therefore cut off from Israelite heritage. Ishmael became Abram's heir after his initiation into the new covenant which prescribed circumcision and patriliny. With his exogamous marriages, Esau also cut his descendants off from membership in the matrilineal descent group of his parents, but he allied himself to Abram's group by marrying one of Ishmael's daughters. Jacob maintained membership in the matrilineal endogamous group of his mother and to a certain extent continued to honor the group's traditions. After Rachel's death he blessed two of her grandchildren in non-patriarchal order, Ephraim over Manasseh,[80] but it was his own twelve sons who formed the patriarchal confederacy.

I think it apparent that the generations known to us as the Early Hebrews were members of a matrilineal social order in which women and men held equally responsible positions within the group. Women enjoyed extensive participation in decision-making within their matrifocal community and were concerned with the marriage ties of their children, which may have represented political alliances; they were deeply involved as educators because they were associated with religious orders that afforded them a measure of power on earth, linked as it was to cosmic power.

Sarah and Rebekah's association with Pharaoh and Abimelech has been attributed to their beauty (Gen. 12:11, 14 and 26:7); in reality the two women participated in significant international interactions with the kings on the order of political alliances, as we shall see in the following chapters.

PART TWO
RELIGIOUS IMPLICATIONS

"Everyone Who Hears Will Laugh With Me" (Gen. 21:6)

In Part I we found that the matriarchs were women of authority and position in a social system different from what has been claimed for them. But that is only half the story. This second part will show that not only were the women held in greater esteem in their society than has previously been recognized, but in addition, the matriarchs had a special position connected to the religious aspects of early Israelite culture. As we continue our analysis, it becomes apparent that the matriarchs Sarah, Rebekah, and Rachel were associated in an important way with a religious order. So little evidence remains in the biblical texts that it is impossible to specify what religious order this might have been, or what rank the matriarchs held. I will refer to the women as "priestesses," but we cannot determine whether our understanding of the term has any relation to the function the matriarchs may have exercised. What we can detect is that some of their decisions, as reported in the texts, are in accord with those made by women of certain religious orders in the ancient Near East.

Because the functions of, and attitudes toward women in religion have changed over the centuries, it is of utmost importance to establish the Genesis narratives within a historical context, particularly with regard to the religious offices of the matriarchs.

The Priestess, the Sacred Prostitute and Sarah

Ancient Mesopotamian priestesses at the beginning of the third millennium B.C.E. were highly regarded in their office as *en* during a ceremony known as the Sacred Marriage (*hieros gamos*), in which they were looked upon as the Goddess incarnate. Sometime during the third millennium, the priest-king was incorporated into the ritual of the *hieros gamos* as the personification of the God and was deified dur-

71

ing his lifetime. By the second millennium the status of the participants had changed to that of god and priestess. The Sacred Marriage
ritual continued to be practiced in Babylonia well into the sixth century B.C.E., when King Nabu-naid installed his daughter as *en* of Ur. It is
during this latter period that the *en* began to be regarded as a sacred
prostitute or harlot.

The women who enacted the role of the holy bride in the ritual of
the *hieros gamos* — which, incidentally, was practiced at certain times
from Egypt to Anatolia — were highly revered and respected in their
communities. To refer to them as "sacred prostitutes" is sacrilegious.
It is not easy for us, with our present moral codes, to envision the customs acceptable in Old Babylonian times. Obviously, it is difficult to
look upon what we now term "sacred prostitution" with an objective
eye, any more than we could accept a present-day king or president
entering into a ritual marriage with a priestess (were one available). A
prostitute is a woman who offers her body to indiscriminate sexual intercourse for hire; *šarrat-é-ki-ùr* (queen of the reed hut, the title given
to the Goddess Ninlil of Nippur) was hardly indiscriminate in her sexual relations, nor was she for hire. In fact, it seems incongruous to
suggest that a *prostitute* was involved in a sacred *marriage*. Nevertheless the Hebrew narrators transformed *zonah* and *qadeshah*, originally
holy women, into common harlots.[1]

It is essential to bear this in mind in the following chapters as it becomes apparent that Sarah, in her capacity as priestess, officiated in
the ritual of the Sacred Marriage on various occasions. The social and
political implications of her religious participation in the ceremony
are difficult to define, but envisioning her status as a woman of religion produces a marked departure from the traditional exposition of
the narratives.

Sarah's religious office has a direct bearing on the conception of
Isaac. The matriarch herself laughed at the thought of her impending
pregnancy, and she laughed again later when the child was born.
"Everyone who hears will laugh with me," she said.

The consequences of a priestess having a child seems to have varied
at different periods in ancient Mesopotamia. According to custom in
the historical period in which the event occurred, the child grew up
claiming the divinity of its mother or was exposed to the elements and
left to its fate.

In order to understand the situation of the biblical matriarchs, it is
important, then, to try to establish whether the time of their stories
was as early as 3000 B.C.E. the Jemdet Nasr period, or closer to the Old
Babylonian period, a thousand years later.

RELIGIOUS IMPLICATIONS

The Jemdet Nasr Period

W.F. Albright suggests that the Terah migration took place during the third quarter of the twentieth century B.C.E. Ephraim A. Speiser and Harry M. Orlinsky are inclined to set it in the seventeenth to fifteenth centuries, during the height of the Hurrian influence.[2] These dates are deduced from data in the narratives relating exclusively to the patriarchs.

However, I believe that some of the stories in which the matriarchs figure prominently in biblical tradition have their origin in remote times and places in the Near East, before the advent of city-states with their defense walls, before centralized governments with their need and greed of acquisition of land and slaves — before, in fact, the general use of writing.

The earliest written records in the Near East were found at a site in Uruk (present-day Warka) in what is usually called the Uruk IV stratum, the date of which is tentatively set at about 3200 B.C.E.[3] Intelligible archaic transcriptions on clay tablets have been found from the late proto-literate period, ca. 3100–2900 B.C.E., which is generally referred to as Jemdet Nasr (and corresponds to the Uruk III–II stratum). The tablets contain what can be understood as the "economic" texts and texts that consist simply of fish, birds, animals, plants, and gods — a kind of primitive lexicon, H.W.F. Saggs suggests.[4]

Not until the end of the Jemdet Nasr period, however, in what are known as Early Dynastic periods (ca. 2900–2400 B.C.E.), is the writing intelligible to us. During this period a people called the Sumerians come into prominence; city-state organization is due to them.

In this Early Dynastic period, a time of transition from open village to walled cities, from a society organized around a theocratic, socialist temple community to a hierarchial state with a king at its head, there was also a change in the status of women. It is in this early transitional stage in human history that I would like to place some segments of the proto-historical records of Genesis. Just as the status and functions of women have changed dramatically in the past one or two thousand years, they changed also in ancient times in a similar span of time.

It would be presumptuous to believe that we can pinpoint the period in which our principal characters lived without hard archaeological evidence to support it. What we can do is examine both the social setting as described in the biblical records, and a period in history in which conditions seem to be similar. Let us compare the Jemdet Nasr period and that of Canaan as described in the Bible.

73

SARAH THE PRIESTESS

1. The fourth millenium B.C.E. was a moderately peaceful age in which wars and raids were not unknown but were not constant and did not dominate human existence.[5] Fortified settlements were few (e.g. Jericho) in the Near East, and evidence of warfare is lacking in most areas. It seems to have been a rare time of idyllic peace in human history.[6]

1. Except in Gen. 14, which is ascribed to an isolated source, the patriarchs of Genesis are not depicted as hero-warriors confronting enemies — whether armies, deities, or monsters (as with Gilgamesh who heroically slays the "ferocious giant" Humbaba). They are mainly concerned with God and family.

2. Early human settlements were primarily made up of a network of small open villages, and it was not until Early Dynastic I (ca. 2900 B.C.E.) that village populations in various regions sought protection behind walls. This period ushered in the fortification of cities.

2. The biblical principals appear to live in small open villages. There are two allusions to a town gate, but in these passages the text suggests that all the people of the town were present in one place, an indication of a small population. (Gen. 19:1-4; 23:10,18)

3. According to Frankfort and others,[7] in pre-dynastic society political power resided in a general assembly that decided upon action in an emergency and chose an officer for the duration of the emergency. As time went on an officer chosen as leader in a specific situation would be disinclined to relinquish his position of prestige once the threat had been dealt with, and would seek ways to perpetuate it. It is possible too that once the cities flourished and increased in number, the threat of an emergency was rarely absent. This trend led to the office becoming an enduring institution. The chosen officer, the *en*, came to be understood to be the leader of a political institution: the term lugal ("great man") was applied to him. The first occurrence of this term, which we interpret as "king," is found in tablets from Ur, dating from Early Dynastic I (ca. 2900 B.C.E.)[8]

3. Abram is depicted as being called (to office?) during an emergency to counter an attack by the "kings" of the north who came to raid the cities of the plains (Gen. 14:1-24). Discovery of material from Ebla suggests that Genesis 14 and Genesis 18:16 through 19:29 could correspond to the third millenium. An example of decision making by an assembly in a time of emergency is found in Genesis 23, in which Abram negotiates with the "children of Heth" as *nasi*, a term designating an official who has been "elevated" in rank, in or by an assembly.

4. In proto-literate periods or earlier (fourth millennium B.C.E.), supernatural power was experienced as

4. Worship of a deity is connected to the symbolism of a sacred tree in Gen. 21:33, in which Abram plants a

a revelation of an in-dwelling spirit, a power at the center of something that caused it to be and thrive and flourish.[9] Trees were held by the ancients to contain such an in-dwelling spirit. Mountains that were revered as the "dwelling-place of the gods" were essentially the mysterious center of activity of superhuman powers.

tamarisk at Beer-sheba and invokes the name of Yahweh. The heights in the land of Moriah (Gen. 22:2) is a mountain on which sacrifice is offered to a deity. El Shaddai means God of the mountain (or breast).

I have attempted to describe what we know of the proto-literate period and relate this to the life of the principals in the Genesis narratives because I believe that the matriarchs held eminent positions as religious functionaries that would have been difficult for a woman to attain in later times.

There are many difficulties in this attempt to relate the matriarchs' activities to those of women of the ancient religions in order to make clear the position of the biblical women. My equating Sarah with a Mesopotamian priestess does not mean that I think she is necessarily of Sumerian or Akkadian origin.

The problem of the origin of the biblical ancestors is not within the scope of this book. But according to the text (Gen. 11:31), Terah's family originated in Mesopotamia, and whether they were Sumerians, Akkadians, or immigrant Semites from somewhere else, they must certainly have been influenced by the religion and culture surrounding them.

In the time between 3000 B.C.E., the Jemdet Nasr period, and ca. 1500 B.C.E., the Hurrian period in Nuzi (cited by Speiser), where can we place the Genesis narratives? Or, to put it another way, when did Sarah live? The more authoritative stature of the matriarchs, and the indications that earlier Sumerian codes were more concerned with the well-being of women than were later Babylonian or Assyrian laws,[10] suggests an earlier date than the often-proposed sixteenth century B.C.E. in which to place the matriarchal narratives. Unfortunately, we cannot come to any definite conclusions about the source(s) used by authors J, E, and P. We can only surmise that the original source(s) for the narrative texts must have contained a much more complete picture of the lives of the matriarchs than the stories we now have.

In the chapters that follow I have chosen to use what we know of ancient priestesses (i.e., female members of religious orders in the ancient Near East) to serve as models in explaining the roles and activities of the matriarchs of Genesis. Our sources are images in the form of figurative art, carvings, relics, paintings, and so on, and inscriptions on clay tablets, sherds or stelae — relics about five thousand years old.

The main objective of this part of my investigation is to show that many of the enigmatic biblical passages that have been all but impossible to explain become intelligible if the women are understood to have held religious offices and to have functioned importantly in that connection within the community.

PLATE 8. Cuneiform inscriptions on clay tablets began to appear in the late proto-literate period, ca. 2800–2400 B.C.E. This tablet comes frm Ur, the birthplace of Sarah. *(The University Museum, University of Pennsylania.)*

V

RELIGION IN THE ANCIENT NEAR EAST

Religion permeated the lives of the ancient Near Eastern peoples. It is evident in their monuments, buildings and archives. Cities had patron deities, and individuals looked to personal gods and goddesses for advice and protection. In the Old Babylonian period great temple compounds were constructed to house the deities and their consorts, their numerous attendants and temple officials, their archives and their wealth. Religious centers gained or lost importance as the political winds shifted, as when Nanna-Sin, the tutelary God of Ur, was "carried off" by the invading Elamites in the Ur III period (2006 B.C.E.) in an effort to divest him of power.

Part of the record we have from the middle of the third millennium B.C.E. is a striking example of the effect of a political upheaval on the religious interests of a region, described in a poem written by a woman who was at once princess, priestess, and poet.[11] Enheduanna (*see* Plate 9), the daughter of Sargon of Agade, was an *en* of Ur and Uruk, ancient centers of Sumerian religion. She was also the author of an impressive literary record, still recognized centuries after her death. Her father Sargon, ruler of Kish and founder of Agade in the north, successfully laid claim to the kingship of Ur and Uruk in the south and at once assumed the religious titles and functions of Lugalzagesi, the deposed ruler. Sargon then installed his daughter as high priestess and "bride" of the moon god Nanna at Ur. With this act he initiated a new and cultically critical institution, with the possible intent of publicly minimizing his own political ambitions. In the poem Enheduanna tells of a usurper of the southern cities banishing her to the steppe and turning over the function of *en* to a candidate of his own.[12] Enheduanna, a devotee of the Goddess Inanna, pleads with the Goddess to expel the usurper. Her father, Sargon, suppressed the rebellion late in his reign, and the rebels acknowledged Ishtar (the Akkadian name of Inanna) as deity. In his politico-religious reformation, Sargon equated the Sumerian Inanna to the Akkadian Ishtar to lay the foundations for a united empire of Sumer and Akkad.[13] This very brief summary should suffice to show the influential position which an *en* was able to attain in the middle of the third millennium B.C.E.

Apart from the position of *en*, the title given to the person we would understand as high priest or priestess, there were numerous other positions held by men and women who were the religious functionaries of Mesopotamian society. Unfortunately, little more than the titles are known to us at present, and specialists in the field often disagree on interpretations of their functions. There is a Sumerian title of *lukur*, for example, and a later, presumably equivalent Akkadian title *naditu* — but the functions of the two do not seem to be interchangeable. To further complicate matters, a *naditu* of the God Shamash may not have had the same function as a *naditu* of the God Marduk. A *naditu* of Sippar would not be the same as one of the same title in Babylon, the more so if they were of different periods as well as different regions. In other words, with the sparse evidence available, it is impossible to generalize about the functions of these specialized offices or the customs and traditions applicable to them.

A *naditu* was member of a particular kind of religious group for which we really have no terminology. Neither do we have an exact classification for the *ugbabtu*, the female personnel serving Zababa, tutelary deity of Kish — some of whom, like the *naditu* of Sippar, lived in a cloister.[14] One restriction evidently common to all these offices (including the Sumerian *lukur* of pre-Babylonian times) was that these women were forbidden to bear children.[15] However, some were allowed to be married, so we cannot refer to them as "nuns." The best designation we have at our disposal is "priestess," though it is vague and inexact.

I have chosen widely from ancient documents to give an idea of the functions of religious women because we know so little about them. In later chapters I may use the function of a *naditu* to explain Sarah's behavior in one instance (as in Gen. 16) and that of an *en* to illustrate another aspect (as in Gen. 18), since it is possible that in certain instances or at a particular time, perhaps in another region, the *en* and the *naditu* had the same functions, or perhaps a woman with characteristics of both held a different title entirely. What does seem to hold is that Sarah functioned as an *en* and as a *naditu* under different circumstances in her story.

PLATE 9. Enheduanna and retinue, shown on a limestone disc from Ur, ca. 2300 B.C.E. *The University Museum, University of Pennsylvania.)*

There are repeated references in the following chapters to an alabaster vase (plates 10 and 11) and a trough (plate 15) from the Uruk III period that show scenes which seem to support a hypothesis of an earlier origin (ca. 3000 B.C.E.) for some of the Sarah narratives.

Other evidence supporting the earlier date is the difference between the code of Hammurapi, ca. 1800 B.C.E., and biblical tradition. Paragraph 145 of the code deals with the succession of a man married to a naditu who must remain childless, and reference is made to the priestess's providing her husband with children. But in the biblical text, Sarah (and also Rachel) speaks of providing *herself* with heirs (*see* Chapter IV, above). The biblical narrative seems to reflect an archaic custom which was later amended by the code of Hammurapi. What was previously a woman's interest in heirs and inheritance was transferred to the husband.

PLATE 10. Relief of Goddess Inanna, or a priestess as her earthly embodiment, standing at the entrance to a storehouse or sanctuary, receiving edibles of various kinds from a procession of (naked) men.

Uruk Vase, fourth millenium B.C.E. (*Iraqi Museum,*

80

PLATE 11. From another angle, the upper frieze shows two priestesses within the sanctuary, its boundaries symbolized by ringed bundles, the insignia of the Goddess Inanna, representing doorposts.

Baghdad, Courtesy State Organization for Antiquities.)

The biblical story, then, contains vestiges from a source earlier than that of Hammurapi's code, which was not, in fact, state law, but rather regulations that Hammurapi was making an effort to enforce. That these regulations often proposed to revise ancient tradition can be appreciated when they are compared to the laws of rulers like Ur-Nammu and Lipit-Ishtar, who preceded Hammurapi. They were also intended to unify and reform the city-states of which Hammurapi became sovereign.

Old Babylonian Period (ca. 1800–1700)

Priestesses of the Old Babylonian religious orders were drawn from all classes; they were daughters of royalty and daughters of the humblest families. They formed part of the ecclesiastical community in virtually all ancient religions in the Near East: Sumerian, Akkadian, Hittite, Assyrian, Egyptian, and others.

En was the title given to the highest rank in the Babylonian clergy. The term *en* ("lady" or "lord") applied to both men and women. In this period the position of *en*, the spiritual head of the temple, was generally conceded to the daughter or the sister of the king. It is difficult to determine the qualifications required of these women for their initiation into the various ranks of the clergy. We do know that the women were devoted to the service of a particular deity; women were in the service of gods, men in the service of goddesses. One of the more important functions of the *en* was the participation in a ritual known as the *hieros gamos*, or Sacred Marriage, which had religious and political implications.

Many laws and regulations regarding the clergy as well as business and marriage contracts and autobiographical notes are available to us from antiquity to help reconstruct a picture of some of the ancient priestesses. Of these documents, some throw light on the biblical narratives of Genesis, and show that the matriarchs of Genesis could have belonged to the ranks of a religious order. This is not to say that the matriarchs actually were priestesses but to suggest that some of the enigmatic passages can be better understood in this regard.

It is difficult to estimate at what period priestesses became celibate in the ancient world, but it is interesting to note in this connection that the most powerful Goddess, the one represented by the priestess in the *hieros gamos*, was Inanna (the Semitic Ishtar or Astarte). She was a woman of many lovers (termed husbands only during the Sacred Marriage ritual), and was not married until the God Dumuzi was incorporated into her mythology. She was never a "mother" goddess;

she remained childless. Like Inanna, the priestess was to remain childless also. Only in a much later time are we told that if the priestess should conceive, the child of the sacred union was to be exposed to the elements and left to its fate, which was usually death. (It could be conjectured that the Akedah, the binding of Isaac, which has caused scholars centuries of perplexity, had its origin in the patriarch's effort to comply with this tradition.) Like the Goddess and the priestess, the matriarch Sarah (and possibly Rebekah also) is portrayed as (almost) having sexual relations with kings, even though she remained childless for close to thirty years.

A feature such as childlessness, whether applied to a goddess, priestess, or matriarch, has a definite meaning only in a historical or sociopolitical context.

Religion and Politics

Jacobsen tells us[16] that "in cities where the chief deity was male, as in Ur, the *en* was a woman [Akkadian *entu*], and therefore, while important religiously, did not attain a ruler's position. Whether male and politically important as a ruler, or female and only culturally important, the *en* lived in a building of sacred character, the *Giparu*."

I do not believe that this statement can be applied to an early period, when leaders were chosen on a temporary basis to perform the ritual of the Sacred Marriage for reversing the effect of a catastrophe of nature, or to lead members of the community in defense against raiders (as Abram did in Gen. 14). It seems that in this period the economy of the community was in the hands of religious officials headed by the keeper of the storehouse, the representative of a goddess. The "political" activity of males referred to by Jacobsen was actually only concerned with military exploits. Initially, the economy of the community was directed from the storehouse, the center where surplus produce was gathered and redistributed.

At some point, when constant warfare demanded a permanent leader, the priestess's position as keeper of the storehouse was usurped by a king who became both priest and monarch, so that the offices of military leader and director of the economy were fused in the concept of one over-all ruler, or king. Since it was men and not women who did the warring and who were organizers of the military establishment, women did not become rulers. The economic office formerly held by female religious leaders became relegated exclusively to the religious sphere. Being unable to defend the "storehouse," the women were forced to relinquish their power, but continued for a time to be concerned with the production and administration of food. There is evidence to show that women of high rank played a very active and important role in the economy of the Ur III period.[17]

The practice of agriculture required the observance and eventual recording of astronomical patterns, and these records evolved into a complex calendar system. One of the functions of the calendar system was to advise the community of agricultural developments around which the festivals grew, celebrating the sowing of the seed, the ripening of the grain, the cutting of the barley. At such times oracles were uttered and dreams interpreted, usually by a priestess. (We may recall that Jacob asked his wives to interpret his dream about his flock. It was due to the interpretation of this dream that the family left Paddam-aram and went to Canaan.)

An interesting resemblance to an episode of Sarah's life (recounted in Gen. 18) is shown on an alabaster vase from the Uruk III period (ca. 3000 B.C.E.). The Goddess Inanna, or a priestess as her earthly embodiment, is shown standing at the entrance of a storehouse or sanctuary and receiving edibles of various kinds from a long procession of men (*see* plates 10 and 11). Since the main act at the end of a Sumerian wedding is the "meeting at the gate" and the "opening of the door" to the bridegroom, Jacobsen suggests that the relief on the vase depicts the last phases of *hieros gamos* (Sacred Marriage), which is followed immediately by preparations for its consummation.[18]

An alabaster trough from the same period as the vase bears the image of the storehouse or sanctuary in the form of a reed hut (*see* Plate 15). The scenes on the vase and the trough both include ringed bundles representing doorposts, the insignia of the Goddess Inanna.

In the course of centuries, this abode of the Goddess or priestess changed dramatically. By the end of the third millennium the archaic reed hut, storehouse of the Goddess which had served to avert anxiety over famine, was outgrown and replaced by a thriving commercial venture whose epicenter was the temple complex.

In early Dynastic times, when natural catastrophes such as famine and earthquakes were no longer the cause of migrations and the war leaders were called on to permanently defend the cities from raiders, the *lugal* (literally, "great man") built walls, temples, and ziggurats — imposing monuments that inspired the communities with awe and respect for a centralized government and religion. The reed hut was replaced by an extensive group of buildings, including a very elaborate temple surrounded by side chapels for lesser deities, rooms for the clergy, kitchens, archives, slaughter houses, and many other rooms connected with the worship and service of divinities. In a list of the temple staff of the Goddess Bau in the time of Urukgania (ca 2378–2371 B.C.E.), 736 persons were enumerated.[19] Both men and women formed the staff of the temples, and their influence over the community grew as the king's position strengthened.

The Sacred Marriage

With the changes on the sociopolitical scene came changes in the rituals.

At one stage in the development of her office, the priestess was regarded as the Goddess incarnate and needed no intermediary to help transmit her utterances or will. The chief function of the priest, on the other hand, was to act as mediator or interpretor between the deity and the worshippers; he obtained guidance for the people in the affairs of daily life.[20]

As military-political and economic power were joined in the king, the heroic acts and deeds of the powerful rulers were listed with the intricate economic records kept of the taxes (in the form of produce) exacted from the people. In time, the *lugal,* or king, was himself inducted as *en* priest and took part in the Sacred Marriage, first as consort and ultimately as god.[21] According to Frankfort,[22] it may well be that only those kings were deified who had been commanded by the Goddess to share her couch. About the time of the Ur III period (ca. 2100 B.C.E.), liturgy of the dying and resurrecting God Dumuzi (Tammuz of the Bible) was introduced into the New Year Festival (an important occasion in which the Sacred Marriage took place). Eventually the divine bridegroom (the king) was identified with the God.[23]

In late Babylonian and Assyrian periods, the Enuma Elish, an epic of creation in which the God Marduk destroys his grandmother, the Goddess Tiamat, and so becomes supreme ruler of the gods, was also incorporated into the drama, of which the *hieros gamos* had then become but a small phase. The essential meaning of the *hieros gamos* remained the same, although local beliefs produced regional varieties. With the inclusion of local epics the local deities became the principals, bestowing fertility on the animal and vegetable produce of their region.

The mystic marriage was understood to take place in the *gigunu,* the reed hut atop the ziggurat, and the principals were deities. It was believed that fertility of flocks and grain throughout the land (i.e., region) depended on the stupendous mysteries that were enacted in this holy place. When the rites were performed in the *gipar,* a temple shrine of the Goddess "on earth," it was some particular natural catastrophe, such as prolonged drought, that the ritual was presumed

PLATE 12. Model of a Sumerian shrine. Clay figurine from Nippur, showing the God in the doorway. *(University Museum, The University of Pennsylvania.)*

to avert by appeasing the deity.[24] A consecrated priest was appointed bridegroom (it is not known exactly how the Goddess intimated her choice). Only after performing a series of intricate duties, requiring special garments, the recital of penitential prayers, libations, and sacrifices, could the bridegroom direct his humble petition to the Goddess (priestess) to predict his fate. If the oracular reply was favorable, he was led to an anteroom of the wedding chamber, where he was seated on a throne opposite the enthroned Goddess (priestess). "A crown was placed on his head and a scepter of righteousness in his hand. Having been thus exalted to the status of a god, he was qualified to participate in the succeeding phases of the sacred drama as if he were indeed the divine consort of the goddess."

"In the course of hundreds of years, as the king cemented his position of power in the religious sphere, the stately ritual that had been followed with scrupulous precision was transformed into a beautiful allegorical mime, from which all realism was purged away."[25] But the rite that originated in prehistoric times was maintained with only temporary lapses throughout three millennia.

VI

ORACULAR SHRINES AND TRADING CENTERS

Sarah and Abram are both associated with many places during their lifetimes, but as discussed in previous chapters, some places were more importantly related to the matriarch than to the patriarch, and this distinction is directly connected to the occupations of the people involved. Ur and Mamre are significant to the story of Sarah; Haran and Beer-sheba to Abram.

Abram was connected to trade or negotiation centers. Sarah, however, was linked exclusively to centers where she could perform religious functions — in particular Mamre, a grove of terebinths where Sarah spent most of her life.

The terebinth (*see* Plate 13) is a small deciduous tree native to the Mediterranean region, the source of the earliest form of turpentine. Ben Sirach eloquently evokes its beauty in a poem:

> Like a terebinth I spread out my branches,
> and my branches are glorious and graceful.
> (Eccles. 24:16)

The terebinth and oak were both sacred trees in ancient Canaan. According to Robert Graves, terebinth groves are associated with Asherah.[26]

So the narrated incidents in the matriarch's life took place on consecrated ground. Abram chose Mamre as Sarah's permanent place of residence. But what of other sites mentioned in the biblical account? What of Shechem, Bethel, Damascus? Were they significant?

Shechem, Navel of the Land

The picture given us in Genesis is that of Abram wandering from Ur to Haran and throughout Palestine with his family, his tents, and

PLATE 13. Terebinth tree *(Pistacia terebinthus).* The terebinth and the oak were both sacred trees in ancient Canaan. Mamre, where Sarah spent most of her life, was a grove of terebinth trees. *(Photo by Dennis Baly.)*

his sheep, settling in one place for a while and then moving on to another.

Since the discovery of the city of Ur by Sir C. Leonard Woolley, the pastoral image of Abram has changed somewhat. According to Woolley, this city was a sophisticated urban environment. As citizen of a great city, Abram (and therefore Sarah also) was the inheritor of an ancient and highly organized civilization.[27] On this basis, the picture of Abram began to be revised. W.F. Albright said that he "suddenly realized that all the places where Abraham is said to have resided were caravan centers or stations,"[28] and he mentions Ur, Haran, Damascus, Shechem, Bethel, and Hebron as such centers. However, all these places were also religious centers or shrines, some of which were associated with sacred trees. (Gen. 12:6; 12:18; 18:1; 21:33.)

The first place on Abram's and Sarah's route in Canaan that the scribes found worth including in the story was Shechem, the site of an oracle-bearing tree, the terebinth of Moreh (Gen. 12). (This implies that other places where they may have stopped were not considered important, were a mere "passing through.") Beneath the boughs of the sacred tree an oracle revealed, for the first time, the meaning of the departure from Mesopotamia: "I will give this land to your off-spring."

Shechem was the center of terebinth veneration and ritual obser-vance in the second millennium B.C.E., and was known as the "Navel of the Land" (Judges 9:37). It was also the site of the Diviner's Oak. In the Authorized Version of the Bible, the words for oak and terebinth are sometimes interchangeable, but these trees, the terebinth and the oak, made a sacred pair in Palestinian religion.[29]

According to E.O. James, the shrine at Shechem can be compared to Delphi, the famous oracular shrine in Greece. It was also regarded as the center of the earth, with its *omphalos,* or navel stone, in the ady-tum of Apollo's temple, where the Pythia gave her oracles.[30] It was through the Pythia, the prophetess of Apollo, that the deity directed how worship and ritual were to be conducted, and clarified ancestral customs. The deity's oracular decrees also bestowed on colonists a ti-tle of possession of the land they occupied,[31] in much the same man-ner as the deity of the sacred terebinth at Moreh bestowed the land on Abram. The prophetess was an inspired figure, giving utterance to di-vine revelations which were the will of the deity. Like the Mesopota-mian *naditu* and the Cumaean sibyl, her office was so sacred that she was forbidden to have normal intercourse with her husband and was also subject to a number of taboos.

The sibyls, oracular women of the same genre as the Pythia, were the successors of the prophetic priestess who spread to Greece from Asis Minor in the sixth century B.C.E. During the second century B.C.E. the sibyls infiltrated the Hellenistic Jewish circles at Alexandria and were inspired, it was said, to propagate the faith and teaching of Isra-el among the uninitiated.

The principal function of all seers attached to these sacred shrines was to consult a deity. This did not necessarily include involvement in sacrifice or worship. But the seers had to be in possession of the tech-nical knowledge necessary to give oracular direction, including augu-ry, incubation, the drawing of lots, and divinatory prophecy.[32]

The matriarch Rebekah, whose children struggled in her womb, made an oracular inquiry "of the Lord" and received the typical pro-nouncement in verse.[33]

We cannot state unequivocally that the oracular promise at the tere-binth of Moreh near Shechem in Genesis 12:7 was uttered by the priestess Sarah, but the fact that priestesses were known to give ora-cles and that Abram built the altars supports the view that he visited the holy places for the purpose of receiving oracular direction, possi-bly from Sarah.

Bethel, too, figures prominently in the scriptures as a sacred shrine, with its oracular oak, called Allon-bacuth ("the Oak of Weeping"), under which Rebekah's wet-nurse Deborah was buried (Gen. 35:8). Bethel was the name given to the site by Jacob after El Shaddai (the deity who brought Sarah and Abram to Canaan) in an oracle gave the land (which he first gave to Abram, then to Isaac) to Jacob and his descendants (Gen. 35:11).

Uprooting Asherah

The spirit embodied in a fruit or leafy type tree or grove in the ancient Near East was female, the most popular in Canaan being the Goddess Asherah. Asherah was venerated from Babylonia (as Ashratum) to Ugarit, Southern Arabia (as Atharath), and Egypt. It is not surprising therefore to find Israelite devotion to the Goddess so strongly entrenched in Hebrew religion that her devotees held fast to her worship throughout the periods of judges and kings and well into the sixth century B.C.E.[34] It was not until King Josiah's reign, a hundred years after the invasion of Israel by the Assyrian King Shalmaneser, that this ardent Yahwist reformer had the Asherahs hewn down and burnt, in accordance with the Deuteronomic law: "You shall not plant for yourself an Asherah, any tree, beside the altar of Yahweh your god, which you shall make for yourself." It is not always clear exactly what the Old Testament refers to when it condemns the Asherahs — whether they were trees, wooden poles or columns embedded in the earth, or sculptured images of the Goddess. One statuette, made of earthenware, has in place of legs the form of a tree trunk (*see* Plate 14), as though it too were to be planted in the earth, suggesting that the numinous character of the Goddess within a tree was the original object of veneration. Both Shechem and Bethel were the focus of Asherah worship and it is likely that the sacred trees mentioned in the text were associated with her.

It was at Bethel that Jacob took for his own the God who had appeared to him at the same site twenty years earlier, when he was fleeing from his brother Esau. First, however, he rid his household of "alien" deities, which he buried under the terebinth near Shechem. The people of Shechem were "purified" in a similar way when Joshua, in his old age, exhorted the people to put away their other Gods and incline their hearts to Yahweh of Israel. He made a covenant with the people, wrote it in stone, and set it under the oak near Shechem as a reminder of their promise. This was probably the same oak under which Deborah was buried.

91

PLATE 14. *Teraphim* of Goddess Asherah with base in the form of a tree trunk. Earthenware figurine from Lachish, eighth century B.C.E. (actual size). *(The Metropolitan Museum of Art, Gift of Harris D. Colt and H. Dunscombe Colt, 1934.)*

It is impossible to say to what extent Sarah accepted the numinous character in the sacred tree. She was certainly linked to the terebinth at Shechem, and to the grove of terebinths at Mamre where she spent most of her life. Since the numinous character of the terebinth was female because it was fruit-bearing, it seems only natural that Sarah, in her religious capacity, would have been familiar with the deity within it. She certainly must have known Asherah, who was venerated in her own homeland as well as in Canaan.

It is not my purpose to associate Sarah specifically with Asherah or any other goddess. But it is important to try to evoke the cultural atmosphere in which Sarah and Abram were living. At Beer-sheba Abram planted a tamarisk tree and "called on the Lord." It was at this same tamarisk that Isaac received the oracle of the renewal of the covenant that Yahweh had made with Abram. And Isaac built an altar there. Centuries of purging and eradication by reformer kings and prophets tend to give the impression that Sarah and Abram and their descendants were quite isolated from the influence of the great religions of their times. In fact, it is generally conceded today that the monotheistic cult of Yahweh was not even introduced to the Israelites until the time of Moses. Like their Sumerian, Akkadian, or Canaanite contemporaries, Sarah and Abram sought divine guidance through omens in situations of anxiety or uncertainty.

Albright was probably correct in associating Abram primarily with trading centers. Abram brought wealth from Haran, such a large holding that he and his nephew Lot had to separate, and he negotiated for a well with Abimelech of Gerar, where he planted the tamarisk. But shrines may very well have been located in the heart of trading centers, and the patriarchs would certainly have taken advantage of their location there. The purpose of the biblical narratives, however, is to unfold the spiritual evolution of a people, and it is for this reason that the oracular sites are mentioned.

Sarah traveled — that is, was taken by Abram — from one hallowed place to another. Ur, her birthplace, and Haran were both centers of moon worship and boasted large temple complexes. Once in Canaan she seems never to have set foot on other than holy ground, symbolized by the sacred terebinth, the grove at Mamre being the most significant. Her life, as we shall see, was dedicated solely to those functions with religious implications.

The Burial of Sarah

We have seen that, except for the incidents in Egypt and Gerar, the important events in Sarah's life were connected with the sacred shrine at Mamre, a district of Hebron. It is at Hebron that the matriarch Sarah was buried. A detailed description is given of the location and special features of the burial ground, for which Abram negotiated with the "children of Heth." It is notable that the burial place of Machpelah is Sarah's grave, where her brother-husband was also buried, but not his wives Hagar and Keturah, nor his sons Ishmael, Zimran, Jokshan, Medan, Midian, Ishbak, or Shua. Was this because Hagar and Keturah were only concubines and were not considered worthy of interment in the same resting places as that of the patriarch? After all, their descendants are marginal to the history of the Hebrews. I do not think so. Sarah's son Isaac was also buried there with his wife Rebekah, but of their descendants only Jacob, the chosen of Rebekah, was buried there — not Esau, Isaac's favorite and the firstborn. Leah was also buried in Mamre with her husband Jacob, but not his concubines Zilpah and Bilhah, even though their sons became the eponymous ancestors of the Hebrews, unlike the sons of Hagar and Keturah who did not. It seems clear that the status of the wives of Abram and Jacob directly influenced the status of their offspring. When Sarah demoted Hagar to slave, Ishmael was disqualified as Sarah's successor. Therefore Ishmael was not buried in the cave of Machpelah. Keturah was a concubine of Abram but did not form part of Sarah's heritage, so her story is discounted with a brief notice. The sons of Zilpah and Bilhah, however, must have been acknowledged by Leah and Rachel as their own offspring, just as Ishmael in the beginning was acknowledged by Sarah as her descendant. The fact that Leah and Rachel's handmaids actually gave birth to some of the children was incidental; the offspring were recognized as having been borne by the matriarchs themselves.

To put it differently, had Ishmael's mother not been demoted by Sarah, it would have been he who "built up the house" of Sarah and it would have been he, Ishmael, who would have taken his place in the cave of Machpelah at his death. The status of Bilhah and Zilpah, handmaids of Rachel and Leah, did not change, and their sons could become members of the confederacy of the twelve tribes of Israel as legitimate heirs of the matriarchs.

Abram made no mention of seeking a family crypt when he negotiated for the purchase of the cave.[35] He stated that the plot was for Sarah. It was for Sarah that Abram carefully chose and contracted for the purchase of the burial ground, close to the sacred area in which the matriarch had spent the greater part of her life.

After Sarah's death, the patriarch's story is concluded with the mention of his marriage to Keturah and a notice of the descendants of

Ishmael. (Abram's association with Keturah is an interesting one. The name Keturah means "incense" and Arabian names like those of some of her sons — Zimran, Joskhan, Medan, and Midian — represent, not individual persons, but well known peoples or tribes connected with the incense trade.) The text does not specify the locale in which Keturah and Abram lived, but it was probably in the south where Abram had been living before Sarah's death. Isaac, it will be remembered, took Rebekah to his mother's tent, that is, to Mamre in Hebron, Sarah's place of residence in Canaan. Jacob and Esau were fourteen years old at the time of Abram's death, but the patriarch had no dealings with them, possibly due to his absence from Hebron. All of these points indicate that the remaining part of Genesis, after the death of Sarah, is concerned with her descendants, not Abram's.

The all-important inference is that the burial place at Machpelah is the resting place of Sarah and members of her descent group. Offspring were privileged to be buried there not because they were sons of wives rather than concubines; it is because they were chosen by the matriarchs as successors. Esau was as much a son of Rebekah and Isaac as his brother, but only Jacob, the elect of Rebekah, was buried at Mamre. Only Jacob married, at Rebekah's insistence, within his mother's kinship group; Esau, it will be remembered, married "out," and was therefore disqualified.

The ancestors of the Hebrews are only those whom the matriarchs accepted as members of their descent group.

As Bakan accurately points out, "Not all the offspring of Abraham are Israelites: the Israelites stem only from Sarah. Sarah is more definitely the ancestor of the Israelites than Abraham."[36]

Most cultures attach a great deal of importance to the places in which revered ancestors lived or were laid to rest. The particular burial practices derived from the data in Genesis suggest that Machpelah was an exceptional crypt, carefully chosen by Abram as the resting place for a particular group of people whose function in life had religious significance. It was not simply a family crypt.

The sacred grove of Mamre at Hebron and the grave in the field of Machpelah, facing Mamre, should take their hallowed place in history in remembrance of the matriarch Sarah.

VII

SARAH AS PRIESTESS

In Part I we were able to discern an image of the matriarch Sarah as a woman who commanded a certain authority over the members of her family and household. Sarah emerged as not simply a first wife preoccupied with giving an heir to her husband, but as a woman who was deeply concerned with the fate of the future generations of her own descent group, and whose actions were forcefully directed at preserving a social pattern traditional to that group. Rebekah and Rachel maintained the same interest in the preservation of these traditions in their generations. It also became apparent that the husbands of the matriarchs, who did not always agree with the women, were nevertheless unable to contradict or oppose them.

Sarah's authority, in particular, was not limited to the family or to the domestic sphere. The extent of her influence is intimated in the accounts of her associations with the kings of Egypt and Gerar. These events are not characteristic of the fate of an ordinary first wife, particularly those related to the powerful monarch of Egypt. What difference could it have made to the divine king whether the woman he had taken into his harem was the wife or sister of a mere mortal? A closer look at this story indicates that Sarah enjoyed a specific social standing far removed from the conventional one of a first wife: the status, in fact, of priestess.

On certain occasions the priestess was regarded as Goddess incarnate; her oracles and utterances were those of a divinity. The priest-king, on the other hand, was receiver and transmitter of the commands of the deity.

It may be because of the different functions of these offices that the matriarchs of Genesis, while depicted as having no direct communication with the deity, seem to be cognizant of divine will. It is Abram, for instance, who is told that Sarah will conceive and bear a son, and it is Abram who is advised of the covenant between God and that son. He is also commanded by the deity: "Whatever Sarah tells you, do as she says." This statement is important because it shows that, at least in that instance, Sarah is in a position of authority recognized by the deity, who instructs Abram to continue acknowledging her position.

The inhabitants of Mesopotamia were of varied origins, but the traditions of each region, whether Sumerian or Akkadian, were acknowledged and respected. The biblical ancestors were bound to reflect the customs prevalent in the area in which they lived. Terah, Nahor, Milcah, and Laban never left the Habur region (*see* Map IV); Sarah, Abram, Rebekah, Leah, and Rachel were born and bred in either southern or northern Mesopotamia; Jacob went back as a young man to spend twenty years there. Only Isaac and Esau never left Canaan for the original homes of their kin. Except for Isaac and his sons, all were born in Mesopotamia and exposed to the formative laws and customs of their social environment. Eleven of the twelve eponymous leaders of the tribes of Israel were born in Paddam-Aram. It would seem reasonable to assume that the emigrants carried with them the culture and customs of their native land, and that they would try to maintain, in their new pastoral-nomadic surroundings, the type of life they had brought with them.

If the emigrant families included women who were associated with religious orders in their homeland, the regulations concerning them would have continued to influence their behavior wherever they went.

What religion the matriarchs could be said to have observed during their lifetimes is an unanswerable question. Nevertheless, careful reading of the Genesis narratives does afford us an insight into the spiritual aspect of their existence.

Sarah spent most of her life living in a terebinth grove, Mamre, a district of the ancient town of Kiriath-Arba, later called Hebron. Her child Isaac was said to be divinely conceived by an anthropomorphic deity who visited her at the sacred grove. Sarah very possibly abhorred the ritual of circumcision practiced by Canaanites. She was buried in a double cave, in a field facing the shrine at Mamre. Only those people who had been chosen as successors by the matriarchs were allowed to be buried in her cave.

Rebekah also was associated with a religious order that restricted childbearing. Her marriage was consummated in Mamre at the residence of Sarah, the former priestess, whose son she married. Rebekah presumably spent twenty years at Mamre before she conceived the twins; it was there that she consulted the oracle which supported her claim to continue the institution of ultimogeniture. Finally, Rebekah and Isaac were forced to leave Hebron because of famine in the region. Rebekah had a strange encounter with Abimelech of Gerar, similar to one of Sarah's. It is not clear whether Rebekah returned to Mamre or remained in the region inhabited by the "uncircumcised Philistines."

Isaac, like Abram, had an exchange with Abimelech and Phicol, his chief of troops, about a well. Isaac remained in Beer-sheba, a religious sanctuary at that time. Its tutelary deity was El Olam. Neither Rebekah nor Isaac is mentioned after the sequence in which they send Jacob to Paddam-Aram for a wife, except for the brief notice of Isaac's death and their burial in the tomb of Sarah (Gen. 49:31).

Rachel, like her predecessor Sarah, conformed to Mesopotamian regulations regarding priestesses who were to remain childless and sought progeny through the services of a handmaid. Rachel and Leah were called to the field where Jacob was with his flocks to interpret his dream. A function of priests and priestesses in the Near East was to supply information about current or future events, whether important or trivial, thought to be known only to the deities with whom they were in some way in communication. The sisters' interpretation of the dream gave Jacob permission to flee from their father Laban.

The story of Rachel and the *teraphim* represents the struggle of women in the religious sphere. *Teraphim* were used by the Babylonians for the purpose of divination and oracular prediction (Ezek. 21:21) and were also used ritually by the Israelites in the time of the judges (Judges, 17:5, 18:14, 17, 20). It is possible that Rebekah used *teraphim* when she consulted the oracle. Nuzi contracts have been cited as an explanation for what has been called Rachel's "strange behavior" in taking the images: "In special circumstances property could pass to a daughter's husband, but only if her father had handed over the household gods to his son-in-law as a formal token that the arrangement had the proper sanction." However, the material referred to comes from documents covering the fifteenth and fourteenth centuries.[37] We are here demonstrating that the origin of these stories describes a social setting considerably earlier than that date. And the *teraphim* were not given by the father, Laban, nor taken by Jacob. The impression given in the narrative is that Rachel was taking possession of the *teraphim* in the same way that she claimed the inheritance: by whatever means she could to get them away from her father, with or without the help of her husband, the implication being that she considered them to be her property. The importance of owning *teraphim* can be appreciated in the story of Micah (Judges, 17: 1-13; 18: 1-31), in which sacred images were taken to a new location so that a new sanctuary could be erected there. Rachel may have intended to found a new shrine in Canaan with the *teraphim*.[38] It would seem, then, that Laban was intent upon enforcing the patriarchy and that the matriarch Rachel was obliged to hide her sacred ritual objects from her father. In pursuing them, Laban intended to wrest the *teraphim* from Rachel, who as youngest daughter has been their guardian, and thus dispossess her as spiritual head. Once in possession of the symbols of office, Laban could install himself in her place. But Laban was unable to find the *teraphim*, so Jacob and his wives continued their journey to the home of Jacob's father, Isaac, who was still in Mamre.

It is important to note that the names of the matriarchs Rachel ("Ewe") and Leah ("Wild Cow") are titles of Mesopotamian goddesses. Early settlers revered the powers in the basic economies characteristic of the region.[39] Ninsuna ("Lady of the Wild Cows") was revered by the cowherds along the lower Euphrates; farther north, among the shepherds, she was known as Duttur, the personified ewe.[40] The names borne by Rachel and Leah are the same as the titles held by the Goddess. The imposition of human over nonhuman forms was achieved slowly and with difficulty, so that the older forms (Wild Cow, Ewe) seemingly lurk under the human exterior during the transition. That Rachel's and Leah's names are well known representations of the nonhuman power in goddesses both in Mesopotamia and in Canaan supports the hypothesis of an early period for the narratives of the matriarchs in Genesis.

One of the most important deities in the Fertile Crescent was the Goddess Astarte. Plaques of the Goddess, for instance, were the most common religious objects found in Kiriath-Sepher, the Book City. The matriarch Sarah spent most of her life in the vicinity of this town.

For Sarah, even more than for the other matriarchs, there are major elements in the episodes which are characteristic of a priestess:

1. Sarah's choice of residence at the terebinth of Mamre;
2. her childlessness;
3. the espisodes with Pharaoh and Abimelech;
4. the supernatural conception of Isaac;
5. Sarah's burial in the cave of Machpelah.

Significantly there is no word in biblical Hebrew for "goddess." Instead, the important religions of the ancient Near East are discredited with terms such as "cult," "heathen," and "pagan." Rachel's *teraphim*, for instance, are constantly referred to as "idols." To her, certainly, they were not.

99

Residence of a Priestess

Information about ancient priestesses comes from places that were religious centers in Mesopotamia, like Nippur and Sippar during the Old Babylonian period (ca. 1800–1700 B.C.E.), with institutions called *gagu* (Akkadian term for cloister), which housed a hundred or more *naditu*. A *naditu* was of elevated priestly rank; she could be of royal birth; and the fundamental restriction was that she remain child-less.[41] The term *"gagum"* is also equated with the "house of the *entu.*"[42]

Sarah, as mentioned in chapter VI, seems never to have set foot on other than hallowed ground. Her extended residence at the sacred grove at Mamre implies that either her abode was cloistered, in the sense that she was enclosed or confined to her surroundings, or that it may have functioned as the *gagu* of the *entu*.

Little detail is given in Genesis about the grove at Mamre, other than to mention that the trees were terebinths and that Sarah lived in a tent. But Sarah's tent is a prominent feature in the narratives. If the terebinth grove where Sarah lived was a sacred area, her residence (the tent resembling the abodes of the goddesses) would have been also. In Genesis 18 reference is made to a tent five times in ten sentences: Abram is outside the tent (v. 1, 2); Sarah is inside it (v. 6, 9); and Sarah is at the entrance to the tent with the divine visitor (v. 10). This emphasis on the tent makes it the pivotal point around which the mystery of the annunciation of Sarah's conception takes place. Genesis does not specify what Sarah's tent was like, but it is certainly an abode of significance, seeing that it is mentioned so frequently, is located in a (sacred) grove, and is visited by a deity.

The abode of the Goddess Inanna, shown in relief on the alabaster trough from Uruk (*see* Plate 15) as a reed hut that could easily be described as a tent, will be seen later to be of great significance.

In II Kings 23:7 there is a strange reference to woven houses. Regarding the reformations of Josiah, it states: "he demolished the houses (*batim*) of the *qedeshim* that were in the house of YHWH, where the women wove houses for Asherah." (Since it did not seem likely that women would be weaving houses — the literal translation — scholars have interpreted *batim* to be stolas, hangings, etc.)[43] Asherah was the Goddess who was venerated most by the Israelites in Canaan and whose influence was recorded by them. Since Asherah was identified with the terebinth, Sarah must have been familiar with her symbols.

The houses woven for Asherah in the priests' quarters, mentioned in II Kings, may have had a configuration similar to the Sumerian

PLATE 15. Alabaster trough, possibly used for kneading. *(above)* Relief of reed hut with sprays of greenery and *(below, end of trough)* reed bundles and rosettes, all symbols of the Goddess Inanna. From Uruk. *(London, The British Museum.)*

Goddess's sacred abode (*see* Plate 12) known as the *gigunu*,[44] initially a reed hut adorned with sprays of greenery. The relief on the trough from the Uruk III period (ca. 3000 B.C.E.) illustrates the shrine of the Sumerian Inanna, and shows it to be made of reeds but resembling a tent. Reeds were plentiful in the Mesopotamian marshes and were used as building materials before the mud brick was invented.[45] In the dry region of Canaan, goat's hair was used to make yarn for weaving tents.

It seems reasonable to infer that the women of the temple did weave houses, representations of the sacred abode of Asherah — the woven house of the Canaanite Goddess being comparable to the reed hut of the Mesopotamian Goddess. I suggest that Sarah's tent was not an ordinary tent. It was symbolic of the abode of a goddess and was associated with the mystic functions of a goddess (or her representative).[46]

That the consummation of Rebekah's union to Isaac took place in Sarah's tent takes on particular significance in this respect. It may be due to this extraordinary circumstance that ancient lore reflects its substance: "Isaac took Rebekah to the tent of his mother Sarah, and she showed herself worthy to be her successor. The cloud appeared again that had been visible over the tent during the life of Sarah, and had vanished at her death, and the gates of the tent were opened for the needy, wide and spacious, as they had been during the lifetime of Sarah."[47] In other words, Sarah's tent was a storehouse. The storehouse is basic to the imagery of Inanna; in fact, the Goddess seems originally to have been the personified power of the storehouse.[48] Inanna's grandmother, Ninlil, who was a participant in the Sacred Marriage in Nippur, bore the title *šarrat-é-ki-ùr*, queen of the reed hut. Indeed, the name Sarah may have originated from a title.[49]

The Meaning of Childlessness

One of the most compelling considerations in associating Sarah with a religious order is her childlessness. Sarah, Rebekah, and Rachel are all presented as being initially barren, and it is only through divine intervention that the first two conceive at all. It seems highly unlikely that three generations of women married to patriarchs would be barren. The recurring mention of the barrenness of the matriarchs is especially significant in view of the fact that the primary purpose of marriage in a patriarchal world is to provide a husband's family with male heirs. According to Raphael Patai, "a childless woman would be regarded as being useless for her husband and would be dismissed," and, "the continuation of the marital status with a barren woman was regarded as undesirable and even immoral."[50] Genesis presents both Sarah and Rachel as being anxious for pregnancy, and Isaac had to plead with the Lord on behalf of Rebekah. Decades passed before any of them conceived.

Legal Aspects

There was no one particular law applicable to all *naditu*, in whatever period or region. Initially, it seems, custom or tradition was followed in a particular situation. At some point contracts were drawn up between interested parties — arranging a marriage, for example. We may find two marriage contracts that are basically the same, but because they are individual contracts they include variable details. There is an interesting case in which three marriage contracts are drawn up by the same conjugal pair.[51] The first agreement is between a *naditu* woman and her husband. In the second document a new wife is introduced who is not related to the first wife. In the final contract the husband must again marry both women because their status is changed: the *naditu* has adopted the second wife as her sister. This third contract is for the benefit of the *naditu* wife, since it stipulates that all the children borne or to be borne by the second wife will be the first wife's children also. Her adopted sister is protected in that the *naditu* wife may not repudiate any of the adoptions.

Genesis 16 implies a marriage contract of the same kind as the one sketched out above, in which the second wife has certain obligations toward the *naditu* wife, including siding with her "whether she is on bad terms or good terms" with their husband. In other words, the *naditu* wife has certain jurisdiction over the second wife. Abram tells Sarah (v. 6), "Your maid is in your hands. Deal with her as you think right." This statement by the husband implies a prior agreement between the spouses. Since early contracts are individual and vary in detail, I have chosen to use in my discussion the general law of the well known warrior-reformer, Hammurapi of Babylon.[52]

Hammurapi's codes 137 and 138 are divorce laws, but they differ in that they apply to two different sets of women. Section 138 permits a man to divorce a woman who has not borne any children. Section 137, which refers to women belonging to religious orders, is quite distinct from the divorce law for secular women. This section concerns specifically the *naditu*[53] who has provided heirs for her husband and the *šugetu* (possibly a lay priestess) who has borne them. If divorced, both women could retain their children and would be provided for: the dowry would be returned and also "half the field, orchard and goods, in order that she may rear her children." Once the children were grown, the *naditu* or *šugetu* would receive a portion corresponding to an individual heir. Unlike the regulation (section 138) for secular women, the code does not make any provision for divorcing women without children. Did tradition, custom or unwritten law forbid divorcing women who had no heirs if they were members of a religious order? The fact that a *naditu* not only kept her children if divorced but was also provided for seems to indicate that even in the time of Hammurapi the provision of an heir for the priestess (if she wanted one) was a significant aspect of the regulations she lived by.

The Hammurapi divorce laws make it quite clear that a *naditu* was not envisioned as physically providing the offspring. Section 137 begins: If a man has made up his mind to divorce a *šugetu* (lay priestess) who bore him children or a *naditu* who provided him with children, he shall return her dowry, etc. The terminology is significant: the *šugetu* bears a child, the *naditu* provides one. Furthermore, the codes are explicit as to the *naditu's* method of providing the child. In section 144 we read: If a man has married a *naditu* and that priestess has given a slave-girl to her husband and she bears sons, (if) thereafter that slave-girl goes about making herself equal to her mistress because she has borne sons, her mistress may not sell her; she may put the mark (of a slave) on her and count her with the slave-girls.

A detailed comparison of this code with the narrative in Genesis has been given in a previous chapter and does not require repetition; but the fact that the Babylonian law written specifically for *naditu* women applies so neatly to the episode involving Sarah and Hagar seems to indicate that the childlessness of Sarah was due to a comparable *naditu* status, rather than an organic cause. I would nevertheless like to emphasize that Hagar, Bilhah, and Zilpah were not the slaves of their respective mistresses Sarah, Rachel, and Leah; they were handmaids. The mention of slaves by Hammurapi and the specific attention to the bearing of sons for the husband are indicative of a different social and economic structure than that of the matriarchs who wanted their lineage to be "builded up" by their handmaids for themselves.

Hammurapi was a military man with what seems to have been a policy of military expansion. With Hammurapi's ascension to power came the ascension of his God, Marduk, whose victory over all the gods and goddesses was observed in the myth and ritual celebration of the Babylonian New Year Festival. It is not surprising that the general's reforms begin with "If a man" this or that. A military man might very well demote a handmaid to a slave, particularly if she lacked respect for her superiors or failed to obey orders. And a man of

PLATE 16. With Hammurapi's ascension to power came the ascension of his God, Marduk. In this detail from the stela of Hammurapi erected in the temple of Marduk, the general is seen before the God Shamash, seated on a throne. *(Louvre Museum, Antiquities Orientales; Cliché Musée Nationaux.)*

war would surely have a stake in the gender of the children born in the community. His emphasis on sons is revealing. I have stressed the difference between the Genesis narratives and the Hammurapi codes because they indicate that they belong to different periods in historical and social setting. The status of women within those societies would differ accordingly.

Childbirth Beyond the Age of Childbearing

After perhaps thirty years of marriage, at an age considered beyond the possibility of childbearing, Sarah has a child. Genesis states that Sarah had passed her menopause when she became pregnant, but Patai argues that this is an editorial comment made by pious editors to emphasize the miraculous element in the event.[54]

Rebekah and Rachel also conceive after lengthy periods of childlessness. For Rebekah it was twenty years before her husband "pleaded with the Lord" on behalf of his wife. Leah had borne four sons before Rachel begged Jacob to "Give me children or I shall die" to which Jacob replied, "Can I take the place of God, who has withheld the fruit of the womb from you?" If Rachel is a priestess, God has withheld the fruit of her womb by the stricture against childbearing, and for this reason Rachel, like Sarah before her, and using the same terminology, gave her maid to her husband so that she might be "builded up" by her maid's offspring.[55]

Interestingly, Sarah, Rebekah, and Rachel are all portrayed as conceiving due to divine intervention. Like the Ugaritic priestess, Rachel believed that she could employ the magic power of mandrakes for their aphrodisiacal properties.[56] These women were not ordinary women, disgraced for being barren; they were very special women whose lives were closely connected to the service of a deity who cared for them and to whom, it seems, they had special access in times of need (Gen. 25:22; 30:22).

On Being a Priestess

Sarah's childlessness and her place of residence are described or implied in the Genesis narratives, but she is not made the central figure in the accounts. The stories of Sarah's and Abram's encounters with the rulers, though told in relation to Abram, do centrally concern Sarah. The patriarch is depicted as Sarah's consort, subservient to her and to the kings. As they stand, these episodes are highly enigmatic.

In the following chapters I will try to untangle what is given in the Genesis texts and analyze them from a different perspective than the traditional one. As mentioned previously, all the stories specifically about Sarah, except for the burial, center around the birth of Isaac. I suggest that the episodes with the kings also have a direct bearing on this main theme of Sarah's life, but are only incidental to the principal subject: accounts of the life of a priestess.

That Sarah's beauty is said to be the cause of conflict with the kings is typically patriarchal: a woman's beauty is her only positive attribute. But beauty alone is not sufficient to explain the anger and fear of the rulers (particularly a powerful Egyptian monarch) when they discover the identity of Sarah or the willingness of both rulers to amend the situation by enriching the patriarch with slaves and livestock. However, if the conflict involved a priestess, a woman closely connected with a deity, any human fear is understandable. Ancient kings, even those deified during their lifetimes, were beholden for their power to gods and goddesses.

In Sarah's time, one of the functions of a priestess was to represent a goddess in a ceremony known as the *hieros gamos* (which will be dealt with at length in the following chapters). And since Genesis portrays the conception of Isaac in supernatural terms, there seems to be reason to see Sarah as a woman of a religious order whose specific standing associated her with this sacred ceremony. Consequently, I suggest that the episodes with the kings, the conflict with Hagar and Ishmael, Sarah's childlessness, the supernatural elements in the conception of Isaac, and the detailed description of her burial are all related to the elevated religious status held by Sarah within her own community in Hebron, and, in fact, in any community with which she may have come in contact.

Because of the complexity of the issues, the elements will be dealt with in separate chapters. The reader should envision these episodes about Sarah as taking place in a sophisticated though protoliterate period, that is, before 3000 B.C.E., at about the time the Uruk vase (*see* Plate 11) and the white marble head of a woman (Plate 17) were made. However, as writing was just being developed in this period I have no option but to use later material for any written documentation on the subject.

As mentioned above, most of the information dealing with ancient "priestesses" comes from religious centers in Mesopotamia like Nippur and Sippar. Cuneiform tablets with this data come from the *gagum* (an Akkadian term), institutions which housed four or more *naditus* over the 250 years of the Old Babylonian period (ca. 1800–1550 B.C.E.).[57] In pre-Old Babylonian times, the Sumerian equivalent of the *naditu*, the *lukur*, was radically different from the *naditu* of the Akkadi-

PLATE 17. This white marble head of a woman, found at Uruk (the Erech of Genesis), city of Inanna, was executed in a sophisticated protoliterate period of the fourth millenium B.C.E. *(Iraqi Museum, Baghdad. Courtesy State Organization for Antiquities.)*

an period and did not live in a community like the *gagu* or cloister.[58] Sarah, who did not live in a cloister (at least in Canaan), is in this respect closer to the *lukur* than the *naditu*. The ancient *lukur* and the *naditu* did share one fundamental restriction. They were to remain childless.

Sarah's association with a religious order and non-patriarchal society makes it possible to clarify the episodes in the Genesis narratives as follows:

1. Sarah may have been a(n oracular) priestess.
2. She was married to her non-uterine brother Abram.
3. Once having settled in Canaan, except for visits to Egypt and Gerar she spent her entire life in Hebron, specifically at the shrine of Mamre where she was buried.
4. The narratives in Genesis which refer to Sarah are concerned with the birth of her son Isaac, her heir.
5. Isaac was conceived through supernatural intervention.
6. One of the means of achieving supernatural conception may have been the performance of the Sacred Marriage rite.
7. The episodes with Pharaoh and/or Abimelech and the events at Mamre contain elements which are also found in the *hieros gamos*.
   (These narratives have evolved through various stages of patriarchal development and editing.)

Sarah's possible participation in the *hieros gamos* becomes highly significant for two reasons: (a) it establishes her professional rank within the community, and (b) it creates an exceptional category for her offspring.

VIII

THE HIEROS GAMOS

It is all but impossible for us, at least four millennia later, to recreate the religious climate of the ancient Near East. Nevertheless, from surviving literature and art we can get some sense of the holy ceremony, the *hieros gamos* or Sacred Marriage. "It was by this religious ritual that Inanna, Queen of Heaven, would take the earth-king into 'the sweetness of her holy loins,' and by her cosmic powers ensure the king's powers of leadership and fertility.[59] (Inanna was the most beloved but not the only Goddess to function in this capacity.) It was the responsibility of the *en* (priestess) to determine the qualifications of the aspirant ruler. The Sumerian ideogram of her title, *nin-dingir-ra*, is translated as "Lady who is a deity";[60] she was envisioned as goddess incarnate, whereas the candidate for political office was deified only for and during the ceremony.

In the Sumerian ritual, enacted during the celebration of the New Year (but believed to have taken place on other occasions as well), the Goddess was understood to have descended from heaven "to enter into direct union with the people of Sumer through their earthly king."[61] The ritual proceeded in stages:

Introductory song and declamation (as the Goddess descends).
Ritual bath of Goddess/*en*.
Love songs of participants.
Meeting at the Gate (bringing of gifts).
Consummation of Marriage.
Determination of Goddess/*en* of the destiny of aspirant.

The destiny of the prospective ruler or king depended on his health, stamina, and virility. He was responsible to the deity for the welfare of the land — for instance, the maintenance of irrigation canals on which the fertility of the land depended. The *lugal* was thus accountable for the prosperity of his people; but it was also his duty to ensure that service to the divinities was strictly enforced. One of the king's major duties in this regard was to build and care for sanctuaries.

This chapter will focus on selected artifacts and literature which describe the *hieros gamos*, in order to give the reader a sense of this ceremony. We cannot do justice to the sanctified act of worship without understanding the sexual function basic to its mystery. In addition, both art and literature serve as the structure necessary for the recovery of a completed account of events in Genesis, particularly regarding chapters 12, 18, 20, and 21, which scholars often find enigmatic. The stories of the kings and the mysterious visit of a deity to Mamre can be understood only with prior knowledge of the *hieros gamos*. It must nevertheless be kept in mind that over the centuries, as Mesopotamian kings gained political influence and control, the enormous power invested in the Goddess/*en* was gradually appropriated by them, and the ritual of the Sacred Marriage changed accordingly. The literary accounts of the *hieros gamos* recorded in this period reflect these changes, as the kings began to identify themselves with the God Dumuzi-Amaushumgalanna, whose death and resurrection were incorporated into the rite.

I do not believe that the stories in Genesis can be tied to so late a date because there is no indication that the kings or the visitor to Mamre were in any way related to the Dumuzi, Osiris, or Tammuz mythological figures. Sarah's religious function was to determine the qualifications of the rulers. Any political or religious influence she may have had is apparent in the Genesis narratives only in that both kings, but particularly Abimelech, are considerate of her status, demonstrating a respect which would not have been accorded a conventional wife, and in the fact that these events took place in Egypt and Gerar, away from the matriarch's permanent residence, giving them a distinct international flavor.

The Alabaster Vase

A scene effectively illustrating Genesis 18 can be found on a tall alabaster vase of the Jemdet Nasr period (ca. 2900 B.C.E.), a time when the awesome power of the Goddess was still recognized. The vase was discovered in the Uruk III stratum, and probably belonged to the furnishings of Inanna's temple. There are three rows of friezes (*see* Plate 10; *detail* plate 18), depicting a woman at the entrance of a storehouse or sanctuary, in the act of receiving offerings. The woman has a heavy mane of hair and is wearing a pointed headdress and a horned crown. She is dressed in a plain long tunic. (The usual attire of an *en-*

PLATE 18. "She comes forth like bright daylight in the heat of noon, when good food has been placed in the storehouse of the land." *(Hymn to Inanna).* Detail from Uruk vase, fourth millenium B.C.E. *(Iraqi Museum, Baghdad. Courtesy State Organization for Antiquities.)*

112

priestess was a skullcap with rolled up edges and a long flounced garment [*see* plates 1 and 9].)

The woman is standing in front of two standards of ringed bundles. Behind her in the sanctuary are the figures of two women, both dressed, standing on pedestals, sacrificing and praying (see Plate 11). A procession of naked men carry baskets, ewers, and libation jars containing fruit and drink; the frieze below shows a continuation of the procession: sheep, and a row of ears of barley and palmshoots, above a stretch of water.[62] The first man in the procession, presumably the leader, is wearing a net skirt and is in the act of offering a basket of fruit to the woman. He is followed by two other men carrying fruit and a cloth girdle.

According to Anton Moortgat, "No-one now queries the real meaning of the composite scene. The Goddess Innin herself, or her substitute, the high priestess, is receiving her bridegroom on New Year's day to celebrate the Sacred Marriage. This bridegroom, who is known from later written sources, is the half-mythical King of Uruk, Dumuzi."[63] Thorkild Jacobsen interprets the scene in a similar way: The Uruk vase "dates from the end of the fourth millennium B.C. and depicts the rite of the sacred marriage. At top left, Amaushumgalanna, the god of the date palm, is shown approaching the gate of his bride at the head of a long retinue bearing his wedding gifts. Receiving him, and opening the gate to him is his bride, the goddess of the storehouse, Inanna. Behind her is the sanctuary in her temple with its altar and sacred furniture, including vases."[64] Jacobsen identifies the first male figure as Amaushumgalanna, a name which he interprets as meaning "the one great source [lit. mother] of the date clusters"[65] in the rite which celebrates the Sacred Marriage only (not the god's death and resurrection), presumably because "the date is easily storeable and endures, as opposed to loss in death, as the dry heat of summer yellows the pastures, and lambing, calving, and milking come to an end."

In his cult the God Dumuzi comprised many aspects of "the élan vital of new life in nature, vegetable and animal, a will and power in it that brings it about." Different economies worshipped him in different aspects, each with its own characteristic segment of ritual events.[66]

The description of the scenes of the Uruk vase by Saggs does not go so far as to identify the leader of the procession as Dumuzi/Amaushumgalanna but states that the "band shows men, naked as befitted a worshipper before a deity, bringing offerings to the gods." After describing the Goddess or a priestess representing the God-

113

dess, Saggs goes on to say that the series of bands has been interpreted as relating to the Sacred Marriage at the New Year feast.[67]

The scholars who identify the first worshipper with the God Dumuzi make their assumptions from evidence found in myths and in descriptions of rituals relating to fertility. However, since we have no written records for the Uruk III period in which the alabaster vase originated, we must base our interpretation on figurative evidence alone. The absence of an inscription makes it difficult to confirm the suggestion that the leader of the procession is a king, much less that it is the mythical Dumuzi-Amaushumgalanna. I stress this point because the Sumerian God Dumuzi (identified later with the Babylonian and biblical Tammuz and in Syria with Adonis) was a dying and resurrecting God whose mythology was incorporated into the New Year festival later, at a time when the Sacred Marriage had been relegated to one phase of an eleven-day celebration.[68] Thus Dumuzi was a relative newcomer to the ceremony. Furthermore, the woman and her attendants in the upper relief of the scene on the vase are depicted as fully dressed, befitting a high status, whereas the men are naked. Only consecrated priests were represented in a state of nudity,[69] and the naked man covered by a net has been interpreted as the "Royal Shepherd of [the Goddess] Inanna,"[70] who cared for her flock. Jacobsen identifies the woman on the vase as the Goddess of the communal storehouse, Inanna, whose horned headdress is a symbol which associates her with moon worship;[71] the lunar calendar, and seasonal predictions for agriculture. The gateposts behind her came to be identified with her and became her symbol.[72]

The Ceremony

Who the goddess's consort was originally is unknown, but in the archaic era it was the priest-king who acted as bridegroom in the Sacred Marriage ceremony, consulted the oracle, and was received by his divine bride, who stationed herself between her symbols (the gateposts at the entrance to the sacred *gipar*) and greeted him with a ceremonious embrace.[73] The bridal couple was then joyously conducted into the nuptial chamber, or *gigunu*,[74] where the mysteries of the union took place. Before entering the holy nuptial chamber, the priest-king was seated upon a throne to mark his elevation to the status of royalty and divinity,[75] facing the enthroned Goddess. It was apparently in this room that the wedding pair feasted during the time they remained in seclusion, their food being the omen of abundance which would result from the felicitous union.[76] The future welfare of the whole community depended on the faultless accomplishment of every detail of the ceremony, and it must have been with great joy that the people were notified of the satisfactory fulfillment of the rites. It is not known exactly how the Goddess intimated her choice of bridegroom, but the person to play her consort had to be somebody of prominence and distinction, supposedly revealed to an officiating high priest in a dream.[77] (There seems to be no documentation for this, however.)

The storehouse in which the nuptial mysteries were enacted, a highly revered sanctuary, is depicted on the alabaster trough decorated with reliefs which has survived from the same period as the vase described above, and is also from Uruk. The storehouse is represented by a reed hut crowned on the right and left by ringed bundles, the standard which was the symbol of the Goddess Inanna (see Plate 16).

Although little is known of the ritual content of the ceremony, there is, fortunately, some literary material, composed and redacted in Sumer for use in religious services,[78] directly related to the *hieros gamos*. According to Samuel Noah Kramer, the Sumerians were among the very few peoples who probably invented a system of writing and also developed it into a vital and effective instrument of communication. A good millennium before the Hebrews wrote down their Bible and the Greeks their Iliad and Odyssey, we find a rich and mature literature from Sumer.[79] Kramer describes in detail various literary forms: myths, epic tales, lamentations, and — of particular interest to us — hymns, a carefully cultivated, highly sophisticated art form in Sumer.[80]

A hymn to the Goddess Inanna, well known for its description of the *hieros gamos* ceremony celebrating the union of the Goddess with king Iddin-Dagan of Isin on New Year's Day, gives the reader a feeling of the reverence felt for the Goddess.[81] Because of the consummation of the sexual act in the ritual, commentators identify the priestess as a "sacred prostitute" or "harlot," but these terms do not convey the real function and lofty prestige of the participants in this ceremony.

*Hymn to Inanna**

The hymn[82] commences with a eulogy of Inanna:

1. To the one who comes forth from heaven, to the one who comes forth from heaven, I would say: "Hail!"

---

*This hymn was composed at least eight hundred years after the time of the Uruk vase and does not necessarily describe a ceremony as performed in the Jemdet Nasr period. This particular performance was conducted in Isin, the city-state of which Iddin-Dagan was ruler.

2. To the hierodule who comes forth from heaven, I would say "Hail!"
3. To the great lady of heaven, Inanna, I would say: "Hail!"
4. To the holy torch who fills the heaven,
5. To the light, Inanna, to her who shines like daylight,
6. To the great lady in heaven, Inanna, I would say: "Hail!"
7. To the hierodule, the awe-laden lady of the Anunna gods,
8. To the trustworthy one who fills heaven and earth with light,
9. To the eldest daughter of Su-en, Inanna, I would say "Hail!"
10. Of her loftiness, of her greatness, of her reliability,
11. Of her coming forth radiantly at evening,
12. Of the holy torch which fills the heaven,
13. Of her stance in heaven, like the moon and the sun,
14. From above and below, all the lands know (of these things).
15. To the greatness of the hierodule of heaven,
16. To Innin I would sing.

The hymn then continues with a description of a procession of people including priests and priestesses, who "walk before the pure Inanna." Some make ready for the festivities:

99. The matriarchs who have been summoned,
100. They prepare great quantities of food and drink for my lady.
101. My lady refreshes the land.

The poet then sees the Goddess approach:

111. She comes forth like the moon at night,
112. She comes forth like bright daylight in the heat of noon.
113. When good food has been placed in the storehouse of the land [Plate 18].

The people of the land make numerous offerings to the Goddess of sheep, dates, fruit, beer. Now they make ready for the ritual:

169. They set up a throne for the lady of the palace.
170. The king, the god, sits with her, inside.
171. For the one who determines the fate of all lands,
172. Who oversees the true first day.
173. Who perfects me^{83} on the day of the disappearance of the Moon.

PLATE 19. "On New Year's Day, the day of ritual, they set up a bed for my lady. . . . She makes love with him on her bed." *(Hymn to Inanna.)* Terracotta bed on four legs, believed to be representation of Sacred Marriage. Third millenium B.C.E. *(Collection of Herr Professor Dr. Erlenmeyer, Basle, Switzerland.)*

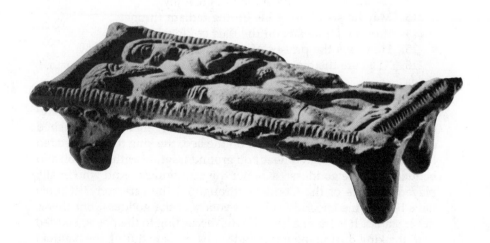

117

174. On New Year's day, the day of ritual.
175. They set up a bed for my lady.

178. They arrange the cover on the outside of the bed.
179. So that they [Inanna and the king] might rest comfortably on "the cover which rejoices the heart."
180. My lady bathes her pure lap.
181. She bathes for the lap of the king,
182. She bathes for the lap of Iddin-Dagan,
183. The pure Inanna washes with soap,
184. She sprinkles cedar oil on the ground,
185. The king approaches her pure lap proudly.
186. He approaches the lap of Inanna proudly,
187. Amaushumgalanna the god lies down beside her,
188. He caresses her pure lap.

191. She makes love with him on her bed [Plate 19].
192. [She says] to Iddin-Dagan, "You are surely my beloved."[84]

The consummation of the sexual act is successful, and this augurs well for the king. Soon after, we find that:

208. The king stretches forth his hand in eating and drinking,
209. Amaushumgalanna stretches forth his hand in eating and drinking.
210. The palace is festive, the king is joyous,
211. The people spend the day in plenty.
212. Amaushumgalanna stands in great joy.
213. May he spend long life on the radiant throne!
214. Proudly [?] he sits on the dais of kingship.
215. He utters the praises of heaven and earth to my lady.
216. "You are the hierodule born with the heaven and the earth."

The Goddess is then celebrated in song by all.

As Kramer explains it, when describing the Sacred Marriage ceremony in which king Iddin-Dagan participated, "Inanna was washed and soaped and presumably laid on the bed; the king then proceeded to the holy lap with lifted head, on ground fragrant with cedar oil and bedded with the goddess." Kramer then continues: "And who finally played the role of the Goddess throughout the ceremony? It must have been some specially selected votary of the goddess, but this is never stated. It is Inanna herself who, according to the poets, bedded with the king during the night and sat by his side during the banquet the following day."[85]

The Sacred Marriage[86] and Genesis

The Sacred Marriage ritual was celebrated when divine intervention was felt to be essential (a) because of some sort of calamity of nature, such as prolonged drought, pestilence, earthquake; or (b) that fruitfulness might be extended to the people and to the whole land.[87] There were two separate phases in the performance of the *hieros gamos:* (1) The Goddess (priestess) forecast the fate of mankind by uttering an oracle foretelling the fate of the priest-king[88] (line 171). This occurred in the *gipar* (sanctuary). (The *gipar*, which in early times had been a simple reed hut, was not a single room but a group of buildings including a dwelling-house for the high priestess or priest and a temple containing an especially sacred chamber known as the *gigunu*.) (2) If the oracle was favorable, the bridegroom's rank was confirmed, and the bridal couple was conducted to the *guenna*, an anteroom resembling a throne room outside the sacred *gigunu*[89] (line 169). The king was seated on a throne facing the Goddess, with a crown placed on his head and a scepter in his hand. "Having been thus exalted to the status of a god, he was qualified to officiate in the succeeding phases of the sacred drama as if he were in very truth the divine consort of the goddess."[90]

An unfavorable oracular pronouncement was not the only cause of communal disaster for a priest-king and his people. Any unworthiness on the part of the king, any error in his performance of the long and complicated ritual, might prejudice the whole ceremony and bring down curses instead of blessings on himself and therefore on his people as well.[91]

The features of the Sacred Marriage ritual just described are not meant to portray an entire performance at any particular time. Only those elements are included which are also apparent in the three episodes in Genesis — Sarah's encounter with Pharaoh (Gen. 12); the appearance of three mysterious visitors at Mamre (Gen. 18); and Sarah's association with Abimelech of Gerar (Gen. 20). Some notable correlations evident are the following:

GENESIS	SACRED MARRIAGE RITUAL
1. The famine was severe in the land.	Drought; calamity of nature.
2. The Lord afflicted Pharaoh and his household with mighty plagues on account of Sarah (Gen. 12:17).	Effect of unfavorable oracle.
3. The Lord closed fast every womb of the household of Abimelech because of Sarah (Gen. 20:18).	Effect of unfavorable oracle.

119

4. You are to die because of the woman you have taken (Gen. 20:3).	Unfavorable oracle.
5. Is anything too wondrous for the Lord? I will return to you at the time when life is due, and Sarah shall have a son (Gen. 18:14).	Favorable oracle.
6. They said to him, "Where is your wife Sarah?" And he replied, "There in the tent" (Gen. 18:9).	The words for "shrine" (*gigunu*) and "sanctuary" (*gipar*) are both composed with the word *gi* ("reed") and mean a reed construction, hut, shrine. The latter part of the word is a picture of an older sort of house with slanted sides and with a conical top.[92] The *gipar* was the traditional residence of the priestess. (Plate 12)
7. Sarah was listening at the entrance of the tent, which was behind him (Gen. 18:10).	The "Opening of the Gate" was part of the formalized ritual of the Sacred Marriage during the New Year festival.[93]
8. Then the *Lord* said to Abram (v. 13), Is anything too wondrous for the *Lord?* (v. 14).	The king is raised to the stature of a *God.*

The characteristics of the Sacred Marriage ritual given above are exclusively from Mesopotamian sources. But let us also consider an Ugaritic source from a text which, as explained by C.H. Gordon, [94] is divided by a scribal line into two sections, of which the first part, he says, is essentially of masculine interest: "The bard opens with the declaration that he sings of the *dramatis personae:* the bride [the Goddess] *Nikkal,* the groom Yarih[95] — the Moon, and Hrhb the King of Summer who acts as intermediary to arrange the match. The time is a fitting one: when the sun goes down and moon rises. The wedding is indicated *because the bride-to-be is destined to bear a son."* The Ktrt are informed of the situation for they are to celebrate joyous occasions like marriages in song. The intermediary (the King of Summer) is instructed to procure the bride for whom Yarih is ready to pay the price of *a thousand shekels of silver,* gold, etc. (cf. Gen. 20:16). Gordon also explains that the text is that of a *hieros gamos.*[96]

The Ugaritic text contains two elements in it that are important: (1) Nikkal the moon Goddess and bride is destined to have a son; and (2) the bridegroom, the moon God Yarih, pays, among other things, a thousand shekels of silver. These two elements can be found in the same sequence in the story of Sarah's encounter with Abimelech of Gerar. In Genesis 18 one of the mysterious visitors to Mamre tells Sarah that she is destined to have a son. Sarah then meets Abimelech and the king gives her a thousand pieces of silver. (It is difficult to assess the value of a thousand silver shekels. The only other mention of silver is the four hundred shekels Abram paid for Sarah's burial site. Either four hundred shekels was very cheap for a piece of real estate or a thousand shekels was the great amount given a priestess for her participation in the *hieros gamos*.) Immediately after Abimelech made the payment (Gen. 20), the Lord took note of Sarah as he had spoken and Sarah conceived and bore a son (Gen. 21). The sequence of events in the Abimelech episode are as follows:

Genesis 18: Annunciation at Mamre
Genesis 19: Interpolation of Sodom and Gomorrah
Genesis 20: *Hieros gamos* with Abimelech
Genesis 21: Birth of Isaac
Genesis 22: The Akedah, binding of Isaac
Genesis 23: Death of Sarah

During her lifetime of service, the priestess would perform more than one Sacred Marriage ritual. Sarah performed two (Pharaoh and Abimelech), and possibly a third (at Mamre), from what we can glean from the biblical texts. The episode with Pharaoh is not quite as clear as the Abimelech story, but Pharaoh too is a vexed king who incomprehensibly gives Abram gifts after he and his household had been afflicted with a plague. We are not told what plague it was, but it was very likely the same "plague" that afflicted the "Philistine" king and his household: barrenness. But this time the wives and concubines and slaves of both kings are barren — not because of their incapacity, but because of his. It was the kings who were barren, not their wives or the women of their households. It was the kings who performed the *hieros gamos*. The ritual was the test and confirmation of a ruler's virility, which would ensure abundance to the land and the people. An unfavorable oracle or any error in the king's performance during the ritual augured disaster for himself and his kingdom.

Once again we can trace the development of the narrative in three stages:

1. The original story.	Enactment of the *hieros gamos* between Sarah and the kings.
2. The original story elaborated with supernatural themes pertaining to ancestor worship.	Description of the *hieros gamos* as told of ancient deities (Inanna/Dumuzi; Nikkal/Yarih), in which themes of virility and a thousand shekels of silver are featured.

3. A toning down of supernatural elements by later scribes.	The story of Abram and Sarah and the kings, in which supernatural intervention indirectly governs their lives.

All the stories of Sarah in Genesis have a direct bearing on the turning point in her life: the birth of her son. If Sarah's association with the kings is interpreted as the *hieros gamos,* there is a direct implication regarding the birth of Isaac.

IX

SUPERNATURAL CONCEPTION

Genesis 18 recounts a truly enigmatic episode in the life of Sarah. This chapter contains many characteristics of a Mesopotamian *hieros gamos* but with the addition of one significant element: the annunciation of conception. It is not clear from the text of Genesis 18 whether conception actually took place at Mamre, but let us review the story in the light of what we have learned about the ceremony.

Traces of the Hieros Gamos in Genesis 18

The Lord appeared at the sacred shrine, the terebinths of Mamre. "I will return to you when life is due," he is reported as telling Abram, "and your wife Sarah shall have a son." Sarah was listening at the entrance of the tent, *which was behind him*. This detail, as inconsequential as it seems, may contain the seed of recollection of a Sumerian ceremony: Thorkild Jacobsen, in describing the original nature of the *gipar* (sanctuary) in which the *en* (priestess) resided, quotes an interesting text: "At the lapis-lazuli door which stands in the *Giparu* she (Inanna) met the *en*[97] at the narrow (?) door," etc. Jabobsen then explains that, during the rite of the "Sacred Marriage," Inanna dressed for her wedding, goes to receive her bridegroom (the God Dumuzi) at the door of the *gipar*: "This opening of the door for the bridegroom by the bride was the main symbolic act of the Sumerian wedding. Inanna then leads the bridegroom into the *Giparu,* where the bed for the sacred marriage is set up."[98] This could suggest that the God was inside the tent with Sarah, or just leaving the tent with his back to the entrance.[99] Had Sarah received the bridegroom (one of the visitors at Mamre) at the door of the *gipar?*

During the episode at Mamre, Sarah does not play the role of a housewife. Abram, for instance, is reported to have told his wife to

123

PLATE 20. Clay figure kneading dough, from ez-Zib; 900–600 B.C.E. *(Palestine Archeological Museum, Jerusalem.)*

knead and make cakes; but it is Abram and a servant who prepare the food and serve it to the visitors, and Sarah's cakes are not mentioned as part of the repast. Sarah remains in the tent or at the entrance throughout the whole sequence.

Other details in Genesis 18 reflect elements of the Mesopotamian Sacred Marriage ritual as we see it depicted in literature and art (the Uruk vase in particular).

HIEROS GAMOS	BIBLICAL PARALLELS
1. Epithets used for the storehouse *(gipar)* in which the Goddess/priestess resided were "holy," "pure"; in archaic texts *gipar* is taken to signify "sacred wood," "grove."[100]	The sequence takes place at the terebinth (sacred) grove of Mamre (v. 1).
2. The first man in the procession on the Uruk vase, presumably the leader, is followed by two other men, his attendants.	He saw three men (v. 2).

3. All the evidence available seems to point to the conclusion that trees were not set up at the entrance to any or every temple but only at the entrance to a temple in which the Sacred Marriage was celebrated.[101]

He waited on them under the tree (v. 8).

4. In preparation for the festivities the bride made provisions of every kind . . . she was assisted in the task by her priests and attendants.[102]

Abram hastened into the tent to Sarah and said, "Quick, three measures of choice flour. Knead and make cakes." (Plate 20.) Then Abram ran to the herd, took a calf, tender and choice, and gave it to a servant-boy to prepare it (v. 7).

5. In the lower frieze of the Uruk vase are depicted sheep (calves would be among cowherders), ears of barley (or wheat for flour) and jars containing drink. (See plates 10,11.)

He took curds and milk and the calf (v. 8).

6. The abode of the Goddess Inanna as shown on the alabaster trough from Uruk is a reed hut, similar to a tent. (See Plate 15.)

They said to him, "Where is your wife, Sarah?" And he replied, "There in the tent."

7. The oracle was delivered which decided the fate of the whole people for the coming year. The bride is destined to bear a son (Ugaritic).

Then one said, "I will return to you when life is due, and your wife Sarah shall have a son."

8. The Goddess/priestess on the Uruk vase is standing in front of two standards of ringed bundles, at the entrance to a temple or storehouse. (See Plate 18.) The storehouse is represented by a reed hut reminiscent of a tent.

Sarah was (listening) at the entrance of the tent.

9. According to an early version of the ritual, the bridal couple was conducted to the nuptial chamber after the oracle.[103]

Now that I am withered am I to have enjoyment, with my husband so old?

10. The priest-king was received by his divine bride . . . and seated upon a throne to mark his elevation to the status of royalty and *divinity*.[104]

Then the Lord said to Abram . . . (v. 13). (This is the first time the visitor is identified as a deity by Abram.)

11. Sexual act has been consummated.

Is anything too wondrous for the Lord? . . . Sarah shall have a son (v. 14).

12. The priestess who performed the Sacred Marriage ritual was to remain childless!

She [Sarah] was frightened (v. 15).

The Question of Paternity

Isaac was conceived through divine agency: "The Lord took note [pqd] of Sarah as he had promised, and the Lord did for Sarah as he had spoken. Sarah conceived and bore a son to Abraham in his old age, at the set time which God had spoken" (Gen. 12:1-2).

As C.H. Gordon points out, the verb paqad is used for a husband visiting his wife for coitus in Judges 15:1.[105] Use of this word in connection with the visit of the Lord to Mamre seems to bring vestiges of a tale of supernatural conception in which a male deity impregnates a human woman, into combination with traces of an account of *hieros gamos*, in which a human male has intercourse with a female deity.

The narrative becomes clearer if we trace its development through the sequence of the three stages described in Chapter I.

1. The original story.	The *hieros gamos* (whether performed at Mamre or not) with Sarah, the priestess representing the incarnation of a Goddess, having intercourse with a priest or king.
2. The original story elaborated with supernatural themes pertaining to ancestor worship.	Supernatural conception with Sarah, a priestess, impregnated by a deity, the change from Goddess to God being more in accordance with the requisites of a patriarchy.
3. A toning down (by later scribes) of supernatural elements in the narratives.	God's intervention in the conception of Isaac by Abram and Sarah, thus divesting Hebrew tradition of the divine descent of their principals.

I think we might say that Sarah, as a priestess, would not have envisioned becoming a mother during her period of service. Had the question arisen after that time, she might have believed that she was beyond the age of childbearing. Sarah does not beg her husband to give her a child, as Rachel later begged Jacob, but asks Abram to "consort with my maid; perhaps I can be builded up through her," as befitted a woman of her position. Let us assume, however, that after her period of service Sarah did consider having a child of her own. Would she have regarded her "brother" (who was also her husband) as the person most suitable to father her child? According to the biblical text, Sarah made no attempt to have her own child. That she had one was an act of God, in whatever sense of the term. Sarah herself laughed at the prospect. Her laughter indicated that she had not been having sexual intercourse with her husband. "Now that I am withered, am I to have enjoyment — with my husband so old?" she questions. With whom, then, did she have intercourse?

Pharaoh, we are told in Genesis 12, took her as his wife. In a similar episode, Abimelech too takes Sarah, but the redactors assure us that the king had not approached her. It would seem, nevertheless, that God knew better than the redactors and told the king in a dream, "You are to die because of the woman you have taken." (Gen. 20:3). That "the Lord closed fast every womb of the household of Abimelech because of Sarah" (Gen. 20:18) must have been the effect of an unfavorable oracle. An unfavorable oracle meant that the king had lost his virility.

I suggest a connection between the sterility of Abimelech in Genesis 20:12 and Sarah's laughter in Genesis 18: ". . . am I to have enjoyment — with my husband so old?" In Hebrew, the word for "my husband," *adoni*, can also be read "God, Lord," *adonay*. The mysterious visitor (whom redactor *J* identifies as YHWH) announces that Sarah will have a child. Since the episode contains so many elements familiar to a Sacred Marriage, we may understand Sarah's expression of incredulity as directed at the age of the groom, not of Abram, her husband. And who was the groom?

Let us consider again the sequence of events:

Genesis 18: Annunciation at Manre
Genesis 19: (Interpolation of) Sodom and Gomorrah
Genesis 20: *Hieros gamos* with Abimelech
Genesis 21: Birth of Isaac
Genesis 22: The Akedah, binding of Isaac
Genesis 23: Death of Sarah

It seems clear that after the annunciation at Mamre came the Sacred Marriage with Abimelech. Abimelech could have been the old man in question, since the oracle doubted his virility, and he was pronounced sterile (Gen. 20:17). But by all accounts, Sarah and the oracle were wrong; true to the prediction at Mamre, Sarah had a child.

It is difficult to tell what role Abram played as consort of Sarah. He certainly administered her holdings; Abimelech says to Sarah "I herewith give your brother a thousand pieces of silver," recalling the thousand shekels given by the God Yarih to the intermediary, the king of Summer, in the Ugaritic text. Was Abram's role no more than an intermediary? It is significant that Abimelech calls Abram "your brother," rather than referring to him as Sarah's husband. (Gen. 20:16.)

According to C.J. Gadd, the *en* priestess who took part in the Sacred Marriage was, in all but a ritual sense, celibate, and possibly even regarded as sexless.[106] The union of Sarah and Abram was probably not looked upon as a marriage in which sexual intercourse played a part, and it would be for this reason that Abram was able to present Sarah to the kings as his sister rather than his wife.

A sexless marriage with Abram would also have made it necessary that for Sarah to be impregnated it would have to be by a deity (or his representative) during the period when she officiated in the marriage rituals. It is difficult to tell what the status was of an *en* or *naditu* who bore a child. That she was expected to remain childless is borne out by the legend of Sargon of Agade, who was exposed at birth to the elements because his mother was a priestess. This, however, was not the case with Gilgamesh before him, or Shulgi who was born three hundred years after Sargon. Both Gilgamesh and Shulgi claimed the Goddess Ninsun as their mother, and were therefore able to claim that they themselves were part divine. Ninsun, the city-goddess of ancient Kullab, was known to give birth to human offspring.[107] Although her husband was Lugalbanda, he was not the father of Gilgamesh. Instead, the Sumerian King List describes the hero's father as "the high priest of Kullab."[108]

In the early *hieros gamos*, the high priestess was the incarnation of the Goddess; she did not merely represent her. A similar tradition, amazingly enough, is found in Jewish legend where God bids Moses to separate from his wife and is queried by the angel Michael as to the purpose of this request. God answered, saying, "Moses has begot children, he has done his duty toward the world. I desire him to unite himself now with the Shekhinah, that she may descend upon the earth for his sake."[109] In the Kabbalah, Shekhinah represents the feminine aspect of the divinity. Moses is then apprised of his destiny.

Divine Attributes

Persons considered divine or holy are sacred beings on whose life the welfare of the community and even the course of nature depends. To these people (or gods) are attributed magical powers, a mysterious energy which, according to its application, may become beneficent or maleficent. These powers are not intrinsic to the holy persons but may be lost through failure to observe strict taboos and rules imposed on them by the community. Thus, Pharaoh celebrated a pre-dynastic ritual, the *Heb-Sed* festival, designed to restore to the monarch his physical strength but it also confirmed his pristine vigor.[110] The pre-occupation with virility is evident in the episode with Abimelech, and was most likely the cause of Pharaoh's vexation too.

Among mortals, qualitative superiority is inherited from a divine parent, earthly heritage from a human parent. Shulgi was conceived by an *en* priestess during the celebration of the Sacred Marriage and the king who embodied the divine bridegroom Nanna, yet he inherited the kingdom from his human father, king Ur-Nammu.

Isaac would inherit divine attributes from his mother,[111] who at the time of his conception was Goddess incarnate; but his heritage he received from his human parents. In Mesopotamia (in a late story about him), Sargon's mother kept her pregnancy secret and was then forced to expose her son to the elements because she was an *en* priestess. The biblical texts tell us nothing of Isaac's infancy or childhood except that he was almost killed by Abram (exposed?), and we are given no reason later for Abram's anxiety lest the steward return with Isaac to Mesopotamia in search of a wife. Was Isaac's birth kept secret at least from the clergy in Mesopotamia? Sargon was saved from his fate by Akki the irrigator, who became his social father; Isaac was saved from a similar fate by Abram. Abram also had the advantage of being the "brother" and husband of the priestess, and would naturally be regarded as the boy's human father.

There is a basic difference between the *en* in her function as Goddess Inanna of Mesopotamia and the priestess as Goddess Nikkal of Ugarit. The former was forbidden to have children; the latter was "destined to bear a son." Could this difference have been the cause of Sarah's incredulity at the annunciation of her conception of Isaac? Sarah laughed, it will be remembered, when the divine visitor said that she would bear a son. Sarah may very well have been unaware of the alternate tradition in the Ugaritic version of the ritual.

I would also like to suggest that, since the scene at Mamre merely hinted at the possibility of sexual activity, whereas the sequence with Abimelech was more specific, Mamre may have been a ritual prelude to the *hieros gamos* with the king of Gerar. In other words, the visitors to Mamre may have included Abimelech himself or a priestly emissary, coming to request Sarah's participation in the Sacred Marriage with the king, or to perform a ritual defloration before the marriage. (In certain Arabic tribes it was customary to give the bride a consummation gift before the first cohabitation after defloration.)[112] The prophecy that Sarah would bear a son and Abimelech's gift of one thousand shekels of silver also echo important elements in the Ugaritic text quoted above.

It seems to me that the sequence at Mamre and the episode with Abimelech must have formed part of the same story. The interpolation of Sodom and Gomorrah and Lot's sexual relationship with his daughters breaks the continuum of a once integrated source. It is only after the annunciation, and after the incident with Abimelech of Gerar and the gift of the thousand shekels that we are told (by the same author, J, who is responsible for the Mamre sequence) that "Sarah conceived and bore a son." The implication is that she did not actually conceive at the annunciation, but later. Later, apparently, was the *hieros gamos* with Abimelech of Gerar.

The Possible Progenitor

The hypothesis of the *hieros gamos* and supernatural conception challenges and raises the question of the identity of Isaac's father. It seems clearly established in Genesis that Sarah was impregnated by a deity. The notice in Genesis 21:2-5 is a later interpolation by the priestly school of scribes *(P)* which succinctly include all the requirements of patriarchal succession: paternity of Abram; naming of child; circumcision of child at age of eight days; and symbolic age of patriarch at time of birth of his son. Abram is nevertheless acknowledged as the father of Isaac by all sources. This is possible if fatherhood is perceived of in two categories: biological and social. If Isaac was a product of the Sacred Marriage and was regarded as divinely conceived, his mother's husband would have been recognized as his human father, just as Jesus is regarded as the son of Joseph though accepted as the son of God. Isaac is therefore the son of Abram.

The actual progenitor of Isaac was probably Abimelech of Gerar. An early Midrash (commentary of the Scriptures) struggled with the paternity of Isaac and resolved it as follows:

> Thus Sarah wandered much: to Pharaoh, to Abimelech. People began to say: "She did not conceive except from Abimelech." The Holy One, blessed by He, said to them: "Let the mouth that speaks lies be stopped. (Ps. 63:12). Wait until she bears and you will see whom he resembles." Instantly the Holy One, blessed be He, commanded the angel who is in charge of the shape of the foetus, and said to him: "Shape him not to be like his mother, but to be like his father, so that everybody should know that he is from nobody else but his father." Instantly he emerged resembling his father. This is why it is said, *Abram begot Isaac.*[113]

But Isaac, like his predecessors Gilgamesh, Sargon, and Shulgi, must have been regarded as part divine. As son of an *en* priestess and a king, deified on the occasion of his conception, Isaac would have been a highly problematic subject to his biographers.

Sarah the Priestess

If Isaac was problematic to his biographers, Sarah was even more so. According to the biblical account the matriarch Sarah lived for ninety years before she conceived and bore Isaac; but the biblical record centers primarily on her child-bearing and rearing. All three matriarchs bore their children late in life, Sarah and Rebekah having one pregnancy and Rachel two. It is interesting that the stories of Sarah and Rebekah were left almost intact, with only a slight change of focus, so that their barrenness (childlessness) necessitated divine intervention (*hieros gamos*) to conform to the patriarchal adage given to Noah: "Be fertile and increase, and fill the earth."

Nevertheless, Sarah spent the major portion of her life as a priestess — not as a mother, not as a wife. We may never know what impact the presence of Sarah may have had on the communities she served, but in her capacity as *en* or *naditu* the issue of her sexual unions was not progeny but bountiful harvests. Sarah's particular obligations in her status as priestess are lost to us, but she lived her life as a religious and (possibly) political professional, and on at least one occasion was paid handsomely for officiating in the ritual of the Sacred Marriage.

In the *hieros gamos* the *en* was the incarnation of a local or patron deity of a city. Did the Goddess Sarah embodied come with her (as did El Shaddai) from Mesopotamia to Canaan? Would a Mesopotamian Goddess have been recognized by Pharaoh and Abimelech? The outstanding characteristics Sarah shared with the goddess of whom she was avatar were childlessness and that she had more than one ritual "husband." In this regard Sarah resembles Inanna, of whom Jacobsen comments:[114] "We see her, in fact, in all the roles a woman may fill except the two which call for maturity and a sense of responsibility. She is never depicted as a wife and helpmate or as a mother." Jacobsen's comment highlights precisely the patriarchal characteristics that were not imposed on Inanna before the end of the third millennium B.C.E., characteristics also absent in the nonpatriarchal milieu of Sarah. (It is worth noting that the patriarchal YHWH has neither spouse nor offspring.)

Sarah lived for thirty-seven years after she became a mother, and was presumably retired from service during that time. Except for the episode that took place at the feast given by Abram when Isaac was weaned, Sarah's experience as a mother is not recorded, even though her son must have been an adult by the time she died.

Sarah died at Kiriath Arba (Hebron) in the land of Canaan at the age of one hundred and twenty-seven.[115] Abram negotiated for her burial place in the presence of "all who entered the gate of his town" (Gen. 23:10), the "children of Heth" (v. 3), also described as "the people of the land" (v. 12). This community must have had some recognition of Sarah's status because the negotiations were not for an individual plot but for Machpelah: "a field with its cave and all the trees anywhere within the confines of that field" (v. 17), which Ephron the owner initially offers to Abram as a gift. The idea that Machpelah was a shrine of particular importance to the community, in deference to the woman who was to be buried there, is reflected in a legend: "The death of Sarah was a loss not only to Abraham and his family, but for the whole country. So long as she was alive, all went well in the land. After her death, confusion ensued. The weeping and wailing over her going hence, was universal."[116]

Sarah the priestess, queen of the holy place in which the Sacred Marriage was solemnized (šarrat-é-ki-ùr)[117] would merit no less than a notable resting place.

PART THREE
CONCLUSIONS

X

THE MEANING OF THE LIFE OF SARAH

What is the meaning of Sarah's life? Is Sarah's message different from Abraham's? I believe so.

The legend of Sarah describes an early tradition which the matriarch struggles to preserve; a non-patriarchal system involved with the forces of nature and their relevance to the community.

This system is diametrically opposed to patriarchality (as presented in Genesis), which emphasizes individuality and the individual whereas non-patriarchality is concerned with the community at large. Biblical patriarchy is contingent upon the precept of blind faith and obedience. (Abram leaves his homeland because his God tells him to; he is willing to sacrifice his son for the same reason.) As Goddess incarnate, the matriarchs maintained a tradition of self-direction. (Sarah has the authority to banish Hagar but Abram accepts the banishment because his God demands that he do so. Rachel takes the *teraphim*, symbols of her office, because in her eyes she has the authority to do so.)

There is a significant difference between the relationship of Sarah with the deity and that of Abram. Sarah is Goddess incarnate (or directly represents a goddess). Abram is the intermediary between his God and his community, and is rewarded for it: "I give the land you sojourn in to you and your offspring to come, all the land of Canaan, as an everlasting possession" . . . but on condition that "I will be their God." (Gen 17:8) Sarah officiates in the *hieros gamos* to appoint a just ruler of the people and insure the fertility of the land and well-being of its people.

The difference between Sarah and Abram can be understood only in the context of a social period comparable to that of the Jemdet Nasr of Mesopotamia. I think the relief on the Uruk vase of the Goddess/

priestess in full regalia at the entrance to her shrine, receiving gifts from a naked ruler/priest, is a perfect illustration of the perception held by the community at Hebron of Sarah and Abram.

Sarah's life as presented in Genesis is indicative of the existence of a social system that was slowly being supplanted by patriarchy. Carol Ochs sees the sacrifice of Isaac as marking the death of the tradition personified by Sarah.[1] I see instead the death of Sarah as marking — not the end of that tradition — but perhaps the beginning of the end. Sarah's separation from her homeland was instrumental in bringing about the change, because it isolated her from the source of her traditions. It took many generations before those traditions were wiped out.

Sarah is symbolic of woman's struggle against a male culture that finally prevailed and eventually subordinated women. How aware was she of the effects of patriarchal encroachment on her own system? We can only imagine what Sarah was thinking and feeling during her interminable years of exile. But we do know that she mustered all her force and energy to banish the offending system (personified by Hagar and Ishmael) from the area in which she lived, and to ensure the continuation of her own tradition through Isaac.

Sarah's story itself gives us only a glimpse of the social tradition and culture she was defending. We know, for instance, that she was of sufficient stature to be respected by kings in communities outside her own. (The kings reprimand Abram, not Sarah.) In other words, Sarah's position was internationally recognized and was not limited to her own community. The matriarch was also held in high esteem by her husband. Abram is solicitous of her favors before their meetings with the kings; he dutifully heeds her request to provide her with a child and accepts Sarah's decision to treat Hagar harshly when the handmaid is insolent to her. Also, Abram's attitude is deferential and subservient to the three mysterious visitors at Mamre, in contrast to Sarah, who argues with one of them.

It seems to me that the Sarah episodes which include her half-brother Abram cannot form part of the same tradition in which the patriarch is the principal. I would tentatively suggest that there were two distinct personalities: one, Sarah's husband and half-brother, whom we call Abram, and another called Abraham. We have seen the careful, courteous, and respectful Abram in the preceding chapters. Is this the same character as the man who mustered his retainers and pursued and defeated Chedorlaomer and his allies?[2] Is this the same person who fell into a trance and with whom the Lord made a covenant with the promise of giving him all the land from Egypt to the Euphrates? Abraham and not Abram would have reproached Abimelech for seizing the well of water. Abraham resided in the "land of the Philistines" a long time, but did Abram? Did Abraham come back from the south to take Isaac from Sarah and attempt to sacrifice him at the command of his God? When, after that, he returned to Beer-sheba, what did he do with Isaac? Did Abraham then return to Mamre to bury Sarah? Genesis makes no mention of Abraham's return: the patriarch is there, mourning the death of his wife.

Although this is pure conjecture, I would like to suggest that the Abraham tradition was different and distinct from the Sarah tradition, in which she had a half-brother/husband named Abram. At some point these two traditions were fused together into what is now our biblical text.

The Abram of the story is, like Isaac, a passive man, easily influenced by the Canaanite patriarchy in which he lived. The name "Abraham," on the other hand, evokes an emotional response built up by centuries of elaboration around the theme of blind monotheistic faith and obedience, of which the patriarch became the symbol.

We get a fuller picture of the Sarah tradition with the accounts of the other matriarchs: Rebekah, Rachel, and Leah. The preservation of blood ties was all-important to these women also. Rebekah marries a member of her descent group even though she has to leave her homeland to do so; however, she becomes "disgusted with her life" because her son Esau marries women native to Canaan. She insists that Jacob choose a wife from among her brother's daughters.

On the surface it would seem that blood ties have something to do with inheritance; Sarah banishes Ishmael so that he will not share in the inheritance with her son Isaac. Rebekah's mother and brother are told of Isaac's inheritance, at the time of her betrothal. Rachel and Leah help pry away their inheritance from Laban as though this were the main conflict between them and their father. However, when Laban pursues them, he is after the teraphim, the family images; no mention is made of stolen wealth. What inheritance were the matriarchs really concerned with?

Sarah's reason for banishing Ishmael is also unclear. Ishmael had been "mocking" Isaac. What connection did Ishmael's mocking have with inheritance? As explained in Chapter III Ishmael's mocking action must have had a religious connotation. There would have been no necessity for Sarah to banish Ishmael if her purpose was merely to disinherit him from material wealth. (Esau was easily disinherited.) Rather, Sarah did not want Ishmael to influence Isaac culturally, and this is why she banished both the boy and his mother. Sarah was a religious woman and a woman of religion, a priestess. Isaac's religious upbringing must have been Sarah's foremost consideration. I do not believe that Sarah's banishment of Ishmael had anything to do with material wealth; it had to do with religious ethics. The rite of circumcision enforced new rules of conduct unacceptable to the priestess.

Rebekah and Rachel were also preoccupied with religious ethics. Why is Rebekah so intent on having Jacob receive his father's blessing rather than Esau? She is not prepared to allow Esau to succeed in the descent line. Is Rebekah concerned with material wealth?

At Rebekah's betrothal the inheritance discussed had been Isaac's material wealth; later, her son Jacob assured himself of a larger portion of the inheritance, that of the firstborn, which Esau had given him in exchange for a bowl of lentils. Rebekah is not interested in that kind of inheritance for Jacob; she is interested in something else, something that the blessing provides, or represents; she is still "disgusted with her life" even after Jacob has received the blessing. Now she insists on sending him to her brother's house for a wife. Jacob chooses Rachel, who is also concerned with religious culture. Rachel takes the *teraphim* when they leave. Her father Laban would not have chased halfway across the country after some statuettes he could have easily replaced; these particular *teraphim* had some important religious significance, and this is why Rachel took them. So Jacob's choice of a religious woman for a wife followed his mother's ambitions for him. It may have been that without the blessing Jacob would not have been acceptable as the husband of a woman of priestly rank, since it is immediately after the blessing that he is sent to be married. It seems evident that the matriarchs were more involved with the perpetuation of their culture and religion in foreign surroundings than their menfolk were.

Nevertheless, the narratives in Genesis certainly trace the genesis of patriarchal religion and culture. Abraham, Isaac, and Jacob do indeed represent an incipient patriarchal tradition among the Hebrews. The extension of that tradition is what our present civilization is all about.

The narratives illustrate the increasing influence patriarchy had on the lives of women over a period of three generations, until the death of Jacob, or approximately three hundred years if the recorded life-spans are taken into consideration.

Patriarchy's greatest asset in its effort to disrupt the matrifocal establishment was mobility. A man's option to move from one location to another with his women and children forced the family to be dependent on him. Significantly the proto-historical portion of the Old Testament commences with the migration of Terah to Haran. Then, as if to emphasize this crucial event, it is sanctified by El Shaddai, who calls Abram with the significant words *lekh lekha*, "walk, go forth" from your native land. Abram's calling was twofold. Leave your matrifocal home, and go to a new land. Once in the new land the same deity makes a covenant with Abram, saying: To your offspring I give this land. Although Abram is not a conquering hero he is the follower of a God who leads him away from an established social setting to a new location which promises possessions and power. It is this same mobility which, generations later, allows Jacob/Israel's sons to spread out and take hold of the land Abram was promised.

Ironically, it was Rebekah's decision to break the rule of matrilocality which sealed the destiny of her gens or descent group. Rebekah left her matrifocal home to marry Isaac in Canaan. Abram sent his servant to bring a wife from the homeland, but he admonished the servant that on no condition must he take Isaac back there. Was this intentional on Abram's part? Sarah was dead. Had the matriarch made arrangements for the betrothal of her son? Would Sarah have insisted on a matrilocal marriage for her son as Rebekah did? Rebekah was very young when she made the decision to leave her mother. It is possible that neither she nor her mother realized the implications for the young woman of living in patriarchal Canaan. Is this why Rebekah was so distressed, why she insisted on a matrilocal marriage for Jacob in contrast to the marriages of her husband Isaac and his favorite, Esau?

The wily Jacob did not live up to his mother's expectations. After twenty years of matrilocal marriage, Jacob must convince his wives to return with him to Canaan. Mobility and possession become the characteristics of Jacob's life. His descendants, the twelve tribes of Israel, claim the land promised to their ancestors.

Interestingly, the matriarchs were not totally discounted: a compromise was found. Endogamy was extended to include all circumcised males, but matriliny remained the only authentic path to membership within the group. Thus, circumcision is not the only requirement for Jewish males; they must also be born of Jewish mothers. And whether the man who impregnates a Jewish woman is circumcised or not, her offspring will automatically be recognized as a Jew, a member of her group.

The narratives of the Sarah tradition represent a non-patriarchal system struggling for survival in isolation in a foreign land. Nevertheless, women of strength emerge from the pages of Genesis, women who are respected by men. Their function in life, though different from that of men, is regarded as equally important to society. Women's participation in society as described in the narratives presupposes a system in which women were able to maintain an elevated professional position into which were incorporated the roles of mother and educator. Just as significantly, these women were in control of their own bodies and their own spiritual heritage.

Sarah, Rebekah, and Rachel, in identification with a goddess, chose to remain childless for decades. They chose to conceive, late in life, because of the circumstances they encountered in exile. They were venerated during their lifetimes as priestesses and as women. It is not clear whether a priestess who became a mother was forced to relinquish her profession. If her progeny was the result of the sexual component in the *hieros gamos*, was her child regarded as the offspring of a goddess, of a mortal woman, or of someone in between represented by a priestess? In other words, did the fact of conception during the ritual of the Sacred Marriage or the fact of birth at a later date establish the status of the mother or the child? In early versions of the ritual the priestess who participated in the *hieros gamos* was thought to be the goddess incarnate; if conception took place the offspring were regarded as part divine. In much later times, a child born of the sacred union was to be exposed to the elements and left to its fate. Sarah's son Isaac, however, was celebrated at a feast given by Abram.[3] Does this mean that Sarah lived at a time when the priestess was regarded as goddess incarnate and her son as semi-divine, as was the case with Gilgamesh? Or was the son's life spared because the priestess was living in safety in exile? What had become of Sarah's status in exile, in the society in which she was living?

How far did Sarah's vision of the society extend? Did she feel that she had been transported to and isolated in a patriarchal future? Did she long for her non-patriarchal homeland? Or did she leave because that social system was changing also? Did she, in fact, have a choice?

These questions and many more can be asked but not answered. But Rebekah's expression of anguish would seem to represent the despair and sorrow experienced by all three matriarchs: "If so, why do I exist?"

Over four thousand years later, this same despair and this same struggle is being experienced by women in both social and religious spheres.

But we are not alone. Sarah is there, standing on the threshold, waiting to be returned to her rightful place in history. Significantly, the title which could qualify the three mothers of Israel, "Priestess," has been totally eradicated from the record. The feminine form of the word for priest (*kohen*) does not appear anywhere in the Hebrew Bible,[4] although it has survived in the form *kahina* in Arabic.

There are still some formidable obstacles to be overcome, but the record of Sarah's life reveals the existence of an alternative system to patriarchy. The social system the three matriarchs defended indicates the presence of a struggle against patriarchy, and of a social structure in which women played a prominent part in religion and culture.

The Sarah tradition gives us an insight into the potential of women's roles to affirm women.

Appendix A

THE TORAH:

RELEVANT CHAPTERS OF GENESIS ACCORDING TO THE MASORETIC TEXT

11 (26) When Terah had lived seventy years, he begot Abram, Nahor, and Haran. (27) Now this is the line of Terah: Terah begot Abram, Nahor, and Haran; and Haran begot Lot. (28) Haran died in the lifetime of his father Terah, in his native land, Ur of the Chaldeans. (29) Abram and Nahor took to themselves wives, the name of Abram's wife being Sarai and that of Nahor's wife Milcah, the daughter of Haran, the father of Milcah and Iscah. (30) Now Sarai was barren, she had no child.

(31) Terah took his son Abram, his grandson Lot the son of Haran, and his daughter-in-law Sarai, the wife of his son Abram, and they set out together from Ur of the Chaldeans for the land of Canaan; but when they had come as far as Haran, they settled there. (32) The days of Terah came to 205 years; and Terah died in Haran.

(Gen. **11**: 26–32)

12 The Lord said to Abram,

Go forth from your native land and from your father's house to the land
that I will show you.
(2)I will make of you a great nation,
and I will bless you;
I will make your name great,
And you shall be a blessing:
(3) I will bless those who bless you,
And curse him that curses you;
All the families of the earth
Shall bless themselves by you.

(4) Abram went forth as the Lord had spoken to him, and Lot went with him. Abram was seventy-five years old when he left Haran. (5) Abram took his wife Sarai and his brother's son Lot, and all the wealth that they had amassed, and the persons that they had acquired in Haran; and they set out for the land of Canaan. When they arrived in the land of Canaan, (6) Abram

passed through the land as far as the site of Shechem, at the terebinth of Moreh. The Canaanites were then in the land.

(7) The Lord appeared to Abram and said, "I will give this land to your offspring," And he built an altar there to the Lord who had appeared to him. (8) From there he moved on to the hill country east of Bethel and pitched his tent, with Bethel on the west and Ai on the east; and he built there an altar to the Lord and invoked the Lord by name. (9) Then Abram journeyed by stages toward the Negeb.

(10) There was a famine in the land, and Abram went down to Egypt to sojourn there, for the famine was severe in the land. (11) As he was about to enter Egypt, he said to his wife Sarai, "I am well aware that you are a beautiful woman. (12) When the Egyptians see you, they will say, 'She is his wife,' and they will kill me, but let you live. (13) Say then that you are my sister, that it may go well with me because of you, and that I may remain alive thanks to you."

(14) When Abram entered Egypt, the Egyptians saw how very beautiful the woman was. (15) Pharaoh's courtiers saw her and praised her to Pharaoh, and the woman was taken into Pharaoh's palace. (16) And because of her, it went well with Abram; he acquired sheep, oxen, asses, male and female slaves, she-asses, and camels.

(17) But the Lord afflicted Pharaoh and his household with mighty plagues on account of Sarai, the wife of Abram. (18) Pharaoh sent for Abram and said, "What is this you have done to me! Why did you not tell me that she was your wife? (19) Why did you say, 'She is my sister,' so that I took her as my wife? Now, here is your wife; take her and be gone!" (20) And Pharaoh put men in charge of him, and they sent him away with his wife and all that he possessed.

(Gen. **12:** 1–20)

13 From Egypt, Abram went up into the Negeb, with his wife and all that he possessed, together with Lot. (2) Now Abram was very rich in cattle, silver, and gold. (3) And he proceeded by stages from the Negeb as far as Bethel, to the place where his tent had been formerly, between Bethel and Ai, (4) the site of the altar which he had built there at first; and there Abram invoked the Lord by name.

(5) Lot, who went with Abram, also had flocks and herds and tents, (6) so that the land could not support them staying together; for their possessions were so great that they could not remain together. (7) And there was quarreling between the herdsmen of Abram's cattle and those of Lot's cattle. — The Canaanites and Perizzites were then dwelling in the land — (8) Abram said to Lot, "Let there be no strife between you and me, between my herdsmen and yours, for we are kinsmen. (9) Is not the whole land before you? Let us separate: if you go north, I will go south; and if you go south, I will go north." (10) Lot looked about him and saw how well watered was the whole plain of the Jordan, all of it — this was before the Lord had destroyed Sodom and Gomorrah — all the way to Zoar, like the garden of the Lord, like the land of Egypt. (11) So Lot chose for himself the whole plain of the Jordan, and Lot journeyed

eastward. Thus they parted from each other; (12) Abram remained in the land of Canaan, while Lot settled in the cities of the Plain, pitching his tents near Sodom. (13) Now the inhabitants of Sodom were very wicked sinners against the Lord.

(14) And the Lord said to Abram, after Lot had parted from him. "Raise your eyes and look out from where you are, to the north and south, to the east and west, (15) for I give all the land that you see to you and your off-spring forever. (16) I will make your offspring as the dust of the earth, so that if one can count the dust of the earth, then your offspring too can be counted. (17) Up, walk about the land, through its length and its breadth, for I give it to you." (18) And Abram moved his tent, and came to dwell at the terebinths of Mamre which are in Hebron; and he built an altar there to the Lord.

(Gen. **13**: 1–18)

16 Sarai, Abram's wife, had bourne him no children. She had an Egyptian maid-servant whose name was Hagar. (2) And Sarai said to Abram, "See, the Lord has kept me from bearing. Consort with my maid; perhaps I shall have a son through her." And Abram heeded Sarai's request. (3) So Sarai, Abram's wife, took her maid Hagar the Egyptian — after Abram had dwelt in the land of Canaan ten years — and gave her to her husband Abram as concubine. (4) And he cohabited with Hagar and she conceived; and when she saw that she had conceived, her mistress was lowered in her esteem. (5) And Sarai said to Abram, "The wrong done me is your fault! I myself gave my maid into your bosom; now that she sees that she is pregnant, I am lowered in her esteem. The Lord decide between you and me!" (6) Abram said to Sarai, "Your maid is in your hands. Deal with her as you think right." Then Sarai treated her harshly, and she ran away from her.

(7) An angel of the Lord found her by a spring of water in the wilderness, the spring on the road to Shur, (8) and said, "Hagar, slave of Sarai, where have you come from, and where are you going?" And she said, "I am run-ning away from my mistress Sarai."

(9) And the angel of the Lord said to her, "Go back to your mistress, and submit to her harsh treatment." (10) And the angel of the Lord said to her,

"I will greatly increase your offspring,
And they shall be too many to count."

(11) The angel of the Lord said to her further,

Behold, you are with child
And shall bear a son;
You shall call him Ishmael,
For the Lord has paid heed to your
suffering.

(12) He shall be a wild ass of a man;

His hand against everyone,
And everyone's hand against him;
And in defiance of all his kinsmen
he shall camp.

(13) And she called the Lord who spoke to her, "You are El-roi," by which she meant, "Have I not gone on seeing after He saw me!" (14) Therefore the well was called Beer-lahai-roi; it is between Kadesh and Bered. (15) And Hagar bore a son to Abram, and Abram gave the son that Hagar bore him the name Ishmael. (16) Abram was eighty-six years old when Hagar bore Ishmael to Abram.

(Gen. **16**: 1–16)

17 When Abram was ninety-nine years old, the Lord appeared to Abram and said to him, "I am El Shaddai. Walk in My ways and be blameless. (2) I will establish My covenant between Me and you, and I will make you exceedingly numerous."

Abram threw himself on his face, as God continued speaking to him, (4) "As for Me, this is My covenant with you: You shall be the father of a multitude of nations. (5)) And you shall no longer be called Abram, but your name shall be Abraham, for I make you the father of a multitude of nations. (6) I will make you exceedingly fertile, and make nations of you; and kings shall come forth from you. (7) I will maintain my covenant between Me and you, and your offspring to come, as an everlasting covenant throughout the ages, to be God to you and to your offspring to come. (8) I give the land you sojourn in to you and your offspring to come, all the land of Canaan, as an everlasting possession. I will be their God."

(9) God further said to Abraham, "As for you, you shall keep my covenant, you and your offspring to come, throughout the ages. (10) Such shall be the covenant, which you shall keep, between Me and you and your offspring to follow: every male among you shall be circumcised. (11) You shall circumcise the flesh of your foreskin, and that shall be the sign of the covenant between Me and you. (12) At the age of eight days, every male among you throughout the generations shall be circumcised, even the homeborn slave and the one bought from an outsider who is not of your seed. — (13) The slave that is born in your household or bought with your money must be circumcised! — Thus shall My covenant be marked in your flesh as an everlasting pact. (14) An uncircumcised male who does not circumcise the flesh of his foreskin — such a person shall be cut off from his kin; he has broken My covenant.

(15) And God said to Abraham, "As for your wife Sarai, you shall not call her Sarai, but her name shall be Sarah. (16) I will bless her; indeed, I will give you a son by her. I will bless her so that she shall give rise to nations; rulers of peoples shall issue from her." (17) Abraham threw himself on his face and laughed, as he said to himself, "Can a child be born to a man a hundred years old, or can Sarah bear a child at ninety?" (18) And Abraham said to God, "Oh that Ishmael might live by Your favor!" (19) God said, "Nevertheless, Sarah your wife shall bear you a son, and you shall name him Isaac; and I will maintain My covenant with him as an everlasting covenant for his offspring to come. (20) As for Ishmael, I have heeded you. I hereby bless him. I will make him fertile and exceedingly numerous. He shall be the father of twelve chieftains, and I will make of him a great nation. (21) But My covenant I will main-

146

tain with Isaac, whom Sarah shall bear to you at this season next year." (22) And when He was done speaking with him, God was gone from Abraham.

(23) Then Abraham took his son Ishmael, and all his homeborn slaves and all those he had bought, every male among Abraham's retainers, and he circumcised the flesh of their foreskins on that very day, as God had spoken to him. (24) Abraham was ninety-nine years old when he circumcised the flesh of his foreskin (25) and his son Ishmael was thirteen years old when he was circumcised in the flesh of his foreskin. (26) Thus Abraham and his son Ishmael were circumcised on that very day; (27) and all his retainers, his homeborn slaves and those that had been bought from outsiders, were circumcised with him.

(Gen. **17**: 1–27)

18 The Lord appeared to him by the terebinths of Mamre; he was sitting at the entrance of the tent as the day grew hot. (2) Looking up, he saw three men standing near him. As soon as he saw them, he ran from the entrance of the tent to greet them and, bowing to the ground, (3) he said, "My lords, if it please you, do not go on past your servant. (4) Let a little water be brought; bathe your feet and recline under the tree. (5) And let me fetch a morsel of bread that you may refresh yourselves; then go on — seeing that you have come your servant's way." They replied, "Do as you have said."

(6) Abraham hastened into the tent to Sarah, and said, "Quick, three measures of choice flour! Knead and make cakes!" (7) Then Abraham ran to the herd, took a calf, tender and choice, and gave it to a servant-boy, who hastened to prepare it. (8) He took curds and milk and the calf that had been prepared, and set these before them; and he waited on them under the tree as they ate.

(9) They said to him, "Where is your wife Sarah?" And he replied, "There, in the tent." (10) Then one said, "I will return to you when life is due, and your wife Sarah shall have a son!" Sarah was listening at the entrance of the tent, which was behind him. (11) Now Abraham and Sarah were old, advanced in years; Sarah had stopped having the periods of women. (12) And Sarah laughed to herself, saying, "Now that I am withered, am I to have enjoyment — with my husband so old?" (13) Then the Lord said to Abraham, "Why did Sarah laugh, saying, 'Shall I in truth bear a child, old as I am?' (14) Is anything too wondrous for the Lord? I will return to you at the time that life is due, and Sarah shall have a son." (15) Sarah dissembled, saying, "I did not laugh," for she was frightened. He replied, "But you did laugh."

(Gen. **18**: 1–15)

19 (15) As dawn broke, the angels urged Lot on, saying, "Up, take your wife and your two remaining daughters, lest you be swept away because of the iniquity of the city." (16) Still he delayed. So the men seized his hand, and the hands of his wife and his two daughters — in the Lord's mercy on him — and brought him out and left him outside the city. (17) When they had brought them outside, one said, "Flee for your life! Do not look behind you, nor stop anywhere in the Plain; flee to the hills, lest you be swept away." (18) But Lot said to them, "Oh no my lord! (19) Please, if you favor your servant, having already shown me so much kindness by saving my life — I cannot flee to the hills, lest disaster overtake me and I die. (20) See, that town there is near enough to flee to; it is such a little place! Let me flee there — it is such a little place — and let my life be saved." (21) He replied, "Very well, I will grant you this favor too, and I will not annihilate the town of which you have spoken. (22) Hurry, flee there, for I cannot do anything until you arrive there." Hence the town came to be called Zoar.

(23) As the sun rose upon the earth and Lot entered Zoar, (24) the Lord rained upon Sodom and Gomorrah sulfurous fire from the Lord out of heaven. (25) He annihilated those cities and the entire Plain, and all the inhabitants of the cities and vegetation of the ground. (26) Lot's wife, behind him, looked back, and she thereupon turned into a pillar of salt.

(Gen. 19: 15–26)

(30) Lot went up from Zoar and settled in the hill country with his two daughters, for he was afraid to dwell in Zoar; and he and his two daughters lived in a cave. (31) And the older one said to the younger, "our father is old, and there is not a man on earth to consort with us in the way of all the world. (32) Come, let us make our father drink wine, and let us lie with him, that we may maintain life through our father." (33) That night they made their father drink wine, and the older one went in and lay with her father; he did not know when she lay down or when she rose. (34) The next day the older one said to the younger, "See, I lay with Father last night; let us make him drink wine tonight also, and you go and lie with him, that we may maintain life through our father." (35) That night also they made their father drink wine, and the younger one went and lay with him; he did not know when she lay down or when she rose.

(36) Thus the two daughters of Lot came to be with child by their father. (37) The older one bore a son and named him Moab; he is the father of the Moabites of today. (38) And the younger also bore a son, and she called him Ben-ammi; he is the father of the Ammonites of today.

(Gen. 19: 30–38)

20 Abraham journeyed from there to the region of the Negeb and settled between Kadesh and Shur. While he was sojourning in Gerar, (2) Abraham said of Sarah his wife, "She is my sister." So Abimelech king of Gerar had Sarah brought to him. (3) But God came to Abimelech in a dream by night and said to him, "You are to die because of the woman that you have taken, for she is a married woman." (4) Now Abimelech had not approached her. He said, "O Lord, will You slay people even though innocent? (5) He himself said to me, 'She is my sister!' Moreover, she said, 'He is my brother.' When I did this, my heart was blameless and my hands were clean." (6) And God said to him in the dream, "I knew that you did this with a blameless heart, and so I kept you from sinning against Me. That was why I did not let you touch her. (7) But you must restore the man's wife — since he is a prophet, he will intercede for you — to save your life. If you fail to restore her, know that you shall surely die, you and all that are yours."

(8) Early next morning, Abimelech called all his servants and told them all that had happened; and the men were greatly frightened. (9) Then Abimelech summoned Abraham and said to him, "What have you done to us? What wrong have I done you that you should bring so great a guilt upon me and my kingdom? You have done to me things that ought not to be done. (10) What, then," Abimelech demanded of Abraham, "was your purpose in doing this thing?" (11) "I thought," said Abraham, "surely there is no fear of God in this place, and they will kill me because of my wife. (12) And besides, she is in truth my sister, my father's daughter though not my mother's; and she became my wife. (13) So when God made me wander from my father's house, I said to her, 'Let this be the kindness that you shall do me: whatever place we come to, say there of me: He is my brother.'"

(14) Abimelech took sheep and oxen, and male and female slaves, and gave them to Abraham; and he restored his wife Sarah to him. (15) And Abimelech said, "Here, my land is before you; settle wherever you please." (16) And to Sarah he said, "I herewith give your brother a thousand pieces of silver; this will serve you as vindication before all who are with you, and you are cleared before everyone." (17) Abraham then prayed to God, and God healed Abimelech, his wife and his slave girls, so that they bore children;

(Gen. **20**: 1–17)

21 The Lord took note of Sarah as He had promised, and the Lord did for Sarah as He had spoken. (2) Sarah conceived and bore a son to Abraham in his old age, at the set time of which God had spoken. (3) Abraham gave his new-born son, whom Sarah had borne him, the name of Isaac. (4) And when his son Isaac was eight days old, Abraham circumcised him, as God had commanded him. (5) Now Abraham was a hundred years old when his son Isaac was born to him. (6) Sarah said, "God has brought me laughter; everyone who hears will laugh with me." And she added.

Who would have said to Abraham
That Sarah would suckle children!
Yet I have borne a son in his old age.

(8) The child grew up and was weaned, and Abraham held a great feast on the day that Isaac was weaned.

(9) Sarah saw the son, whom Hagar the Egyptian had borne to Abraham, playing. (10) She said to Abraham, "Cast out that slave-woman and her son, for the son of that slave shall not share in the inheritance with my son Isaac." (11) The matter distressed Abraham greatly, for it concerned a son of his. (12) But God said to Abraham, "Do not be distressed over the boy or your slave; whatever Sarah tells you, do as she says, for it is through Isaac that offspring shall be continued for you. (13) As for the son of the slave-woman, I will make a nation of him, too, for he is your seed."

(14) Early next morning Abraham took some bread and a skin of water, and gave them to Hagar. He placed them on her shoulder, together with the child, and sent her away. And she wandered about in the wilderness of Beer-sheba. (15) When the water was gone from the skin, she left the child under one of the bushes, (16) and went and sat down at a distance, a bowshot away; for she thought, "Let me not look on as the child dies." And sitting thus afar, she burst into tears.

(17) God heard the cry of the boy, and an angel of God called to Hagar from heaven and said to her, "What troubles you, Hagar? Fear not, for God has heeded the cry of the boy where he is. (18) Come, lift up the boy and hold him by the hand, for I will make a great nation of him." (19) Then God opened her eyes and she saw a well of water. She went and filled the skin with water, and let the boy drink. (20) God was with the boy and he grew up; he dwelt in the wilderness and became a bowman. (21) He lived in the wilderness of Paran; and his mother got a wife for him from the land of Egypt.

(22) At that time Abimelech and Phicol, chief of his troops, said to Abraham, "God is with you in everything that you do. (23) Therefore swear to me here by God that you will not deal falsely with me or with my kith and kin, but will deal with me and with the land in which you have sojourned as loyally as I have dealt with you." (24) And Abraham said, "I swear it."

(25) Then Abraham reproached Abimelech for the well of water which the servants of Abimelech had seized. (26) But Abimelech said, "I do not know who did this; you did not tell me, nor have I heard of it until today." (27) Abraham took sheep and oxen and gave them to Abimelech, and the two of them made a pact. (28) Abraham then set seven ewes of the flock by themselves, (29) and Abimelech said to Abraham, "What mean these seven ewes which you have set apart?" (30) He replied, "You are to accept these seven ewes from me as proof that I dug this well." (31) Hence that place was called Beer-sheba, for there the two of them swore an oath. (32) When they had concluded the pact at Beer-sheba, Abimelech and Phicol, chief of his troops, departed and returned to Philistine country. (33) (Abraham) planted a tamarisk at Beer-sheba, and invoked there the name of the Lord, the Everlasting God. (34) And Abraham resided in the land of the Philistines a long time.

(Gen. 21: 1–34)

22 (20) Some time later, Abraham was told, "Milcah too has borne children to your brother Nahor: (21) Uz the first-born, and Buz his brother, and Kemuel the father of Aram; (22) and Chesed, Hazo, Pildash, Jidlaph and Bethuel" — (23) Bethuel being the father of Rebekah. These eight Milcah bore to Nahor, Abraham's brother. (24) And his concubine, whose name was Reumah, also bore children: Tebah, Gaham, Tahash, and Maacah.

(Gen. 22: 20–24)

23 Sarah's lifetime — the span of Sarah's life — came to one hundred and twenty-seven years. (2) Sarah died in Kiriath-arba — now Hebron — in the land of Canaan; and Abraham proceeded to mourn for Sarah and to bewail her. (3) Then Abraham rose from beside his dead, and spoke to the children of Heth, saying, (4) "I am a resident alien among you; sell me a burial site among you, that I may remove my dead for burial." (5) And the children of Heth replied to Abraham, saying to him, (6) "Hear us, my lord: you are the elect of God among us. Bury your dead in the choicest of our burial places; none of us will withhold his burial place from you for burying your dead." (7) Thereupon Abraham bowed low to the people of the land, the children of Heth, (8) and he said to them, "If it is your wish that I remove my dead for burial, you must agree to intercede for me with Ephron, the son of Zohar. (9) Let him sell me the cave of Machpelah which he owns, which is at the edge of his land. Let him sell it to me in your presence, at the full price, for a burial site."

(10) Ephron was present among the children of Heth; so Ephron the Hittite answered Abraham in the hearing of the children of Heth, all who sat on the council of his town, saying, (11) "No, my lord, hear me: I give you the field and I give you the cave that is in it; I give it to you in the presence of my people. Bury your dead." (12) Then Abraham bowed low before the people of the land, (13) and spoke to Ephron in the hearing of the people of the land, saying, "If only you would hear me out! Let me pay the price of the land; accept it from me, that I may bury my dead there." (14) And Ephron replied to Abraham, saying to him, (15) "My lord, do hear me! A piece of land worth four hundred shekels of silver — what is that between you and me? Go and bury your dead." (16) Abraham accepted Ephron's terms. Abraham paid out to Ephron the money that he had named in the hearing of the children of Heth — four hundred shekels of silver at the going merchants' rate.

(17) So Ephron's land in Machpelah, facing Mamre — the field with its cave and all the trees anywhere within the confines of that field — (18) passed to Abraham as his possession, in the presence of the children of Heth, of all who sat on the council of his town. (19) And then Abraham buried his wife Sarah in the cave of the field of Machpelah, facing Mamre — now Hebron — in the land of Canaan. (20) Thus the field with its cave passed from the children of Heth to Abraham, as a burial site.

(Gen. **23**: 1–20)

24 Abraham was now old, advanced in years, and the Lord had blessed Abraham in all things. (2) And Abraham said to the senior servant of his household, who had charge of all that he owned, "Put your hand under my thigh (3) and I will make you swear by the Lord, the God of heaven and the God of the earth, that you will not take a wife for my son from the daughters of the Canaanites among whom I dwell, (4) but will go to the land of my birth and get a wife for my son Isaac." (5) And the servant said to him, "What if the woman does not consent to follw me to this land, shall I then take your son back to the land from which you came?" (6) Abraham answered him, "On no account must you take my son back there! (7) The Lord, the God of heaven, who took me from my father's house and from the land of my birth, who promised me under oath, saying, 'I will give this land to your offspring' — He will send His angel before you, and you will get a wife for my son from there. (8) And if the woman does not consent to follow you, you shall then be clear of this my oath; but do not take my son back there." (9) So the servant put his hand under the thigh of Abraham his master and swore to him as bidden.

(10) Then the servant took ten of his master's camels and set out, taking with him all the bounty of his master; and he made his way to Aram-naharaim, to the city of Nahor. (11) He made the camels kneel down by the well outside the city, at evening time, the time when women come out to draw water. (12) And he said, "O Lord, God of my master Abraham, grant me good fortune this day, and deal graciously with my master Abraham: (13) As I stand here by the spring and the daughters of the townsmen come out to draw water, (14) let the maiden to whom I say, 'Please, lower your jar that I may drink,' and who replies, 'Drink, and I will also water your camels' — let her be the one whom You have decreed for Your servant Isaac. Thereby shall I know that You have dealt graciously with my master."

(15) He had scarcely finished speaking, when Rebekah, who was born to Bethuel, the son of Milcah the wife of Abraham's brother Nahor, came out with her jar on her shoulder. (16) The maiden was very beautiful, a virgin whom no man had known. She went down to the spring, filled her jar, and came up. (17) The servant ran toward her and said, "Please, let me sip a little water from your jar." (18) "Drink, my lord," she said, and she quickly lowered her jar upon her hand and let him drink. (19) When she had let him drink his fill, she said, "I will also draw for your camels, until they finish drinking." (20) Quickly emptying her jar into the trough she ran back to the well to draw, and she drew for all his camels.

(21) The man, meanwhile, stood gazing at her in silence, to learn whether the Lord had made his errand successful or not. (22) When the camels had finished drinking, the man took a gold nose-ring weighing a half-shekel, and two gold bands for her arms, ten shekels in weight. (23) "Pray tell me," he said, "whose daughter are you? Is there room in your father's house for us to spend the night?" (24) She replied, "I am the daughter of Bethuel the son of Milcah whom she bore to Nahor." (25) And she went on, "There is plenty of straw and feed at home, and also room to spend the night." (26) The man bowed low in homage to the Lord (27) and said "Blessed be the Lord, the God of my master Abraham, who has not withheld His steadfast kindness from my master. For I am on the road on which the Lord has guided me — to the house of my master's kinsmen." (28) The maiden ran and told all this to her mother's household. (29) Now Rebekah had a brother whose name was Laban. Laban ran out to the man at the spring (30) when he saw the nose-ring and the bands on his sister's arms, and when he heard his sister Rebekah say, "Thus the man spoke to me." He went up to the man, who was still standing beside the camels by the spring. (31) "Come in, O blessed of the Lord," he said, "why do you remain outside, when I have made ready the house and a place for the camels?" (32) So the man entered the house. The camels were

unloaded and given straw and feed, and water was brought to bathe his feet and the feet of the men with him. (33) But when food was set before him, he said, "I will not eat until I have told my tale." He said, "Speak, then."

(34) "I am Abraham's servant," he began. (35) "The Lord has greatly blessed my master, and he has become rich: He has given him sheep and cattle, silver and gold, male and female slaves, camels and asses. (36) And Sarah, my master's wife, bore my master a son in her old age, and he has given him everything he owns. (37) Now my master made me swear, saying, 'You shall not get a wife for my son from the daughters of the Canaanites in whose land I dwell; (38) but you shall go to my father's house, to my kindred, and get a wife for my son.' (39) And I said to my master, 'What if the woman does not follow me?' (40) He replied to me, 'The Lord, whose ways I follow, will send His angel with you and make your errand successful; and you will get a wife for my son from my kindred, from my father's house. (41) Thus only shall you be freed from my adjuration: if, when you come to my kindred, they refuse you — only then shall you be freed from my adjuration.'

(42) "I came today to the spring, and I said: O Lord, God of my master Abraham, if You would indeed grant success to the errand on which I am engaged! (43) As I stand by the spring of water, let the young woman who comes out to draw and to whom I say, 'Please, let me drink a little water from your jar,' (44) and who answers, 'You may drink, and I will also draw for your camels' — let her be the wife whom the Lord has decreed for my master's son.' (45) I had scarcely finished praying in my heart, when Rebekah came out with her jar on her shoulder, and went down to the spring and drew. And I said to her, 'Please give me a drink.' (46) She quickly lowered her jar and said, 'Drink, and I will also water your camels.' So I drank, and she also watered the camels. (47) I inquired of her, 'Whose daughter are you?' And she said, 'The daughter of Bethuel son of Nahor, whom Milcah bore to him.' And I put the ring on her nose and the bands on her arms. (48) Then I bowed low in homage to the Lord and blessed the Lord, the God of my master Abraham, who led me on the right way to get the daughter of my master's brother for his son. (49) And now, if you mean to treat my master with true kindness, tell me; and if not, tell me also, that I may turn right or left."

(50) Then Laban and Bethuel answered, "The matter stems from the Lord; we cannot speak to you bad or good. (51) Here is Rebekah before you; take her and go, and let her be a wife to your master's son, as the Lord has spoken." (52) When Abraham's servant heard their words, he bowed low to the ground before the Lord. (53) The servant brought out objects of silver and gold, and garments, and gave them to Rebekah; and he gave presents to her brother and her mother. (54) Then he and the men with him ate and drank, and they spent the night. When they arose next morning, he said, "Give me leave to go to my master." (55) But her brother and her mother said. "Let the maiden remain with us some ten days; then you may go." (56) He said to them "Do not delay me, now that the Lord has made my errand successful. Give me leave that I may go to my master." (57) And they said, "Let us call

the girl and ask for her reply." (58) They called Rebekah and said to her, "Will you go with this man?" And she said, "I will." (59) So they sent off their sister Rebekah and her nurse along with Abraham's servant and his men. (60) And they blessed Rebekah and said to her,

O Sister!
May you grow into
Thousands of myriads;
May your offspring seize
The gates of their foes.

(61) Then Rebekah and her maids arose, mounted the camels, and followed the man. So the servant took Rebekah and went his way.

(62) Isaac had just come back from the vicinity of Beer-lahai-roi, for he was settled in the region of the Negeb. (63) And Isaac went out walking in the field toward evening, and looking up, he saw camels approaching. (64) Raising her eyes, Rebekah saw Isaac. She alighted from the camel (65) and said to the servant, "Who is that man walking in the field toward us?" And the servant said, "That is my master." So she took her veil and covered herself. (66) The servant told Isaac all the things that he had done. (67) Isaac then brought her into the tent of his mother Sarah, and he took Rebekah as his wife. Isaac loved her, and thus found comfort after his mother's death.

(Gen. **24**: 1–67)

25 Abraham took another wife, whose name was Keturah. (2) She bore him Zimran, Jokshan, Medan, Midian, Ishbak, and Shuah.

(Gen. **25**: 1–2)

(7) This was the total span of Abraham's life: one hundred and seventy-five years. (8) And Abraham breathed his last, dying at a good ripe age, old and contented; and he was gathered to his kin. (9) His sons Isaac and Ishmael buried him in the cave of Machpelah, in the field of Ephron the son of Zohar the Hittite, facing Mamre, (10) the field Abraham had bought from the children of Heth; there Abraham was buried, and Sarah his wife. (11) After the death of Abraham, God blessed his son Isaac. And Isaac settled near Beer-Lahai-roi.

(Gen. **25**: 7–11)

(19) This is the story of Isaac, son of Abraham. Abraham begot Isaac. (20) Isaac was forty years old when he took to wife Rebekah, daughter of Bethuel the Aramean. (21) Isaac pleaded with the Lord on behalf of his wife, because she was barren; and the Lord responded to his plea, and his wife Rebekah conceived. (22) But the children struggled in her womb, and she said, "If so, why do I exist?" She went to inquire of the Lord, (23) and the Lord answered her,

Two nations are in your womb,
Two peoples apart while still in your body;
One people shall be mightier than the other,
And the older shall serve the younger.

(24) When her time to give birth was at hand, there were twins in her womb. (25) The first one emerged red, like a hairy mantle all over; so they named him Esau. (26) Then his brother emerged, holding on to the heel of Esau; so they named him Jacob. Isaac was sixty years old when they were born.

(27) When the boys grew up, Esau became a skillful hunter, a man of the outdoors; but Jacob was a mild man, who stayed in camp. (28) Isaac favored Esau because he had a taste for game; but Rebekah loved Jacob. (29) Once when Jacob was cooking a stew, Esau came in from the open, famished. (30) And Esau said to Jacob, "Give me some of that red stuff to gulp down, for I am famished" — which is why he was named Edom. (31) Jacob said, "First sell me your birthright." (32) And Esau said, "I am at the point of death, so of what use is my birthright to me?" (33) But Jacob said, "Swear to me first." So he swore to him, and sold his birthright to Jacob. (34) Jacob then gave Esau bread and lentil stew; and he ate, drank, rose, and went his way. Thus did Esau spurn the birthright.

(Gen. 25: 19–34)

26 There was a famine in the land — aside from the previous famine that had occurred in the days of Abraham — and Isaac went to Abimelech, king of the Philistines, in Gerar. (2) The Lord had appeared to him and said, "Do not go down to Egypt; stay in the land which I point out to you. (3) Reside in this land, and I will be with you and bless you; I will give all these lands to you and to your offspring, fulfilling the oath that I swore to your father Abraham. (4) I will make your descendants as numerous as the stars of heaven, and give to your descendants all these lands, so that all the nations of the earth shall bless themselves by your offspring — (5) inasmuch as Abraham obeyed Me and followed My mandate: My commandments, My laws, and My teachings."

(6) So Isaac stayed in Gerar. (7) When the men of the place asked him about his wife, he said, "She is my sister," for he was afraid to say "my wife," thinking, "the men of the place might kill me on account of Rebekah, for she is beautiful." (8) When some time had passed, Abimelech king of the Philistines, looking out of the window, saw Isaac fondling his wife Rebekah. (9) Abimelech sent for Isaac and said, "So she is your wife! Why then did you say: She is my sister?" Isaac said to him, "Because I thought I might lose my life on account of her." (10) Abimelech said, "See what you have done to us! One of the people might have lain with your wife, and you would have brought guilt upon us." (11) Abimelech then charged all the people, saying, "Anyone who molests this man or his wife shall be put to death"

(Gen. 26: 1–11)

(34) When Esau was forty years old, he took to wife Judith daughter of Beeri the Hittite, and Basemath daughter of Elon the Hittite; (35) and they were a source of bitterness to Isaac and Rebekah.

(Gen. **26**: 34–35)

27 When Isaac was old and his eyes were too dim to see, he called his older son Esau and said to him, "My son." He answered, "Here I am." (2) And he said, "I am, you see, so old that I do not know how soon I may die. (3) Take, then, your gear, your quiver and bow, and go out into the country and hunt me some game. (4) Then make me a tasty dish such as I like, and bring it to me to eat, so that I may give you my innermost blessing before I die."

(5) Rebekah had been listening as Isaac spoke to his son Esau. When Esau had gone out to the country to hunt game to bring home, (6) Rebekah said to her son Jacob, "I overheard your father speaking to your brother Esau, saying, (7) 'Bring me some game and make me a tasty dish to eat that I may bless you, with the Lord's approval, before I die.' (8) Now, my son, listen carefully as I instruct you. (9) Go to the flock and fetch me two choice kids, and I will make of them a tasty dish for your father, such as he likes. (10) Then take it to your father to eat, in order that he may bless you before he dies." (11) Jacob answered his mother Rebekah, "But my brother Esau is a hairy man I am smooth-skinned. (12) If my father touches me. I shall appear to him as a trickster and bring upon myself a curse, not a blessing." (13) But his mother said to him, "Your curse, my son, be upon me! Just do as I say and go fetch them for me."

(14) He got them and brought them to his mother, and his mother prepared a tasty dish such as his father liked. (15) Rebekah then took the best clothes of her older son Esau, which were there in the house, and had her younger son Jacob put them on; (16) and she covered his hands and the hairless part of his neck with the skins of the kids. (17) Then she put in the hands of her son Jacob the tasty dish and the bread that she had prepared.

(18) He went to his father and said, "Father." And he said, "Yes, which of my sons are you?" (19) Jacob said to his father, "I am Esau, your first-born; I have done as you told me. Pray sit up and eat of my game, that you may give me your innermost blessing." (20) Isaac said to his son, "How did you succeed so quickly, my son?" And he said, "Because the Lord your God granted me good fortune." (21) Isaac said to Jacob, "Come closer that I may feel you, my son — whether you are really my son Esau or not." (22) So Jacob drew close to his father Isaac, who said as he felt him, "The voice is the voice of Jacob, but the hands are the hands of Esau." (23) He did not recognize him because his hands were hairy like those of his brother Esau. As he prepared to bless him, (24) he asked, "Are you really my son Esau?" And when he said, "I am," (25) he said, "Serve me and let me eat of my son's game that I may give you my innermost blessing." So he served him and he ate, and he brought him wine and he drank. (26) Then his father Isaac said to him, "Come close and kiss me, my son"; (27) and he went up and kissed him. And he smelled his clothes and he blessed him, saying,

See, the smell of my son
Is as the smell of the field
That the Lord has blessed.
(28) May God give you
Of the dew of heaven and the fat of the earth,
Abundance of new grain and wine.
(29) Let peoples serve you,
And nations bow to you;
Be master over your brothers,
And let your mother's sons bow to you.
Cursed be they who curse you,
Blessed they who bless you.

(30) No sooner had Jacob left the presence of his father Isaac — after Isaac had finished blessing Jacob — than his broher Esau came back from his hunt. (31) He too prepared a tasty dish and brought it to his father. And he said to his father, "Let my father sit up and eat of his son's game, so that you may give me your innermost blessing." (32) His father Isaac said to him, "Who are you?" And he said, "Esau, your first-born!" (33) Isaac was seized with very violent trembling. "Who was it then," he demanded, "that hunted game and brought it to me? Moreover, I ate of it before you came, and I blessed him; now he must remain blessed!" (34) When Esau heard his father's words, he burst into wild and bitter sobbing, and said to his father, "Bless me too, Father!" (35) But he answered, "Your brother came with guile and took away your blessing." (36) [Esau] said, "Was he then named Jacob that he might supplant me?" (37) Isaac answered, saying to Esau, "But I have made him master over you: I have given him all his brothers for servants, and sustained him with grain and wine. What, then, can I still do for you, my son?" (38) And Esau said to his father, "Have you but one blessing, Father? Bless me too, Father!"

(Gen. **27**: 1–38

(46) Rebekah said to Isaac, "I am disgusted with my life because of the Hittite Women. If Jacob marries a Hittite woman like these, from among the native women, what good will life be to me?"

(Gen. **27**: 46)

28 So Isaac sent for Jacob and blessed him. He instructed him, saying, "You shall not take a wife from among the Canaanite women. (2) Up, go to Paddan-aram, to the house of Bethuel, your mother's father, and take a wife there from among the daughters of Laban, your mother's brother. (3) May El Shaddai bless you, make you fertile and numerous, so that you become a community of peoples. (4) May He grant you the blessing of Abraham, to you and your offspring; that you may possess the land where you are sojourning, which God gave to Abraham."

(5) Then Isaac sent Jacob off, and he went to Paddan-aram, to Laban the son of Bethuel the Aramean, the brother of Rebekah, mother of Jacob and Esau.

(6) When Esau saw that Isaac had blessed Jacob and sent him off to Paddan-aram to take a wife from there, charging him, as he blessed him, "You shall not take a wife from among the Canaanite women," (7) and that Jacob had obeyed his father and mother and gone to Paddan-aram, (8) Esau realized that the Canaanite women displeased his father Isaac. (9) So Esau went to Ishmael and took to wife, in addition to the wives he had, Mahalath the daughter of Ishmael, sister of Nebaioth.

(10) Jacob left Beer-sheba, and set out for Haran.

(Gen. 28: 1–10)

29 (10) And when Jacob saw Rachel, the daughter of Laban his mother's brother, and the flock of Laban his mother's brother, Jacob went up and rolled the stone off the mouth of the well, and watered the flock of Laban, his mother's brother. (11) Then Jacob kissed Rachel, and broke into tears. (12) Jacob told Rachel that he was her father's kinsman, that he was Rebekah's son; and she ran and told her father. (13) On hearing the news of his sister's son Jacob, Laban ran to greet him; he embaced him and kissed him, and took him into his house. He told Laban all that had happened. (14) Laban then said to him, "You are truly my bone and flesh."

When he had stayed with him a month's time, (15) Laban said to Jacob, "Just because you are my kinsman, should you serve me for nothing? Tell me, what shall your wages be?" (16) Now Laban had two daughters; the name of the older one was Leah, and the name of the younger was Rachel. (17) Leah had weak eyes; Rachel was shapely and beautiful. (18) Jacob loved Rachel; so he answered, "I will serve you seven years for your younger daughter Rachel." (19) Laban said, 'Better that I give her to you than that I should give her to an outsider. Stay with me." (20) So Jacob served seven years for Rachel and they seemed to him but a few days because of his love for her.

(21) Then Jacob said to Laban, "Give me my wife, for my time is fulfilled, that I may consort with her." (22) And Laban gathered all the people of the place and made a feast. (23) When evening came, he took his daughter Leah and brought her to him; and he cohabited with her. — (24) Laban had given his maidservant Zilpah to his daughter Leah as her maid. — (25) When morning came, there was Leah! So he said to Laban, "What is this you have done to me? Was it not for Rachel that I have been in your service? Why did you deceive me?" (26) Laban said, "It is not the practice in our place to marry off the younger before the older. (27) Wait until the bridal week of this one is over and we will give you that one too, provided you serve me another seven years." (28) Jacob did so: He waited out the bridal week of the one, and then he gave him his daughter Rachel as wife. — (29) Laban had given his maidservant Bilhah to his daughter Rachel as her maid. — (30) And Jacob cohabited with Rachel also; indeed, he loved Rachel more than Leah. And he served him another seven years.

(31) The Lord saw that Leah was unloved and he opened her womb; but Rachel was barren.

(Gen. **29**: 10–31)

30 When Rachel saw that she had borne Jacob no children, she became envious of her sister; and Rachel said to Jacob, "Give me children, or I shall die." (2) Jacob was incensed at Rachel, and said, "Can I take the place of God, who has denied you fruit of the womb?" (3) She said, "Here is my maid Bilhah. Consort with her, that she may bear on my knees and that through her I too may have children." (4) So she gave him her maid Bilhah as concubine, and Jacob cohabited with her.

(Gen. **30**: 1–4)

(22) Now God remembered Rachel; God heeded her and opened her womb. (23) She conceived and bore a son, and said, "God has taken away my disgrace." (24) So she named him Joseph, which is to say, "May the Lord add another son for me."

(Gen. **30**: 20–24)

31 (3) Then the Lord said to Jacob, "Return to the land of your fathers where you were born, and I will be with you." (4) Jacob had Rachel and Leah called to the field, where his flock was, (5) and said to them, "I see that your father's manner toward me is not as it has been in the past; but the God of my father has been with me. (6) As you know, I have served your father with all my might; (7) but your father has cheated me, changing my wages time and again. God, however, would not let him do me harm. (8) If he said thus, 'The speckled shall be your wages,' then all the flock would drop speckled young; and if he said thus, 'The streaked shall be your wages,' then all the flocks would drop streaked young. (9) God has taken away your father's livestock and given it to me.

(10) "Once, at the mating time of the flocks, I had a dream in which I saw that the he-goats in the flock, as they mated, were streaked, speckeld, and mottled. (11) And in the dream an angel of God said to me, 'Jacob!' 'Here,' I answered. (12) And he said, 'Note well that all the he-goats in the flock which are mating are streaked, speckled, and mottled; for I have noted all that Laban has been doing to you. (13) I am the God of Beth-el, where you anointed a pillar and where you made a vow to Me. Up, then, leave this land and return to the land of your birth.' "

(14) Then Rachel and Leah answered him, saying, "Have we still a share in the inheritance of our father's house? (15) Are we not reckoned by him as outsiders? For he sold us and then used up our purchase price. (16) Truly, all the wealth that God has taken away from our father belongs to us and to our children. Now then, do just as God has told you."

(17) Thereupon Jacob put his children and wives on camels; (18) and he drove off all his livestock and all the wealth that he had amassed, the livestock

in his possession that he had acquired in Paddan-aram, to go to his father Isaac in the land of Canaan.

(19) Meanwhile Laban had gone to shear his sheep, and Rachel appropriated her father's household idols, (20) Jacob kept Laban the Aramean in the dark, not telling that he was fleeing, (21) and fled with all that he had. Soon he was across the Euphrates and heading toward the hill country of Gilead.

(22) On the third day, Laban was told that Jacob had fled. (23) So he took his kinsmen with him and pursued him a distance of seven days, catching up with him in the hill country of Gilead. (24) But God appeared to Laban the Aramean in a dream by night and said to him, "Beware of attempting anything with Jacob, good or bad."

(25) Laban overtook Jacob. Jacob had pitched his tent on the Height, and Laban with his kinsmen encamped in the hill country of Gilead. (26) And Laban said to Jacob, "What did you mean by keeping me in the dark and carrying off my daughters like captives of the sword? (27) Why did you flee in secrecy and mislead me and not tell me? I would have sent you off with festive music, with timbrel and lyre. (28) You did not even let me kiss my sons and daughters good-by! It was a foolish thing for you to do. (29) I have it in my power to do you harm; but the God of your father said to me last night, 'Beware of attempting anything with Jacob, good or bad.' (30) Very well, you had to leave because you were longing for your father's house; but why did you steal my gods?"

(31) Jacob answered Laban, saying, "I was frightened at the thought that you would take your daughters from me by force. (32) But anyone with whom you find your gods shall not remain alive! In the presence of our kinsmen, point out what I have of yours and take it." Jacob, of course, did not know that Rachel had appropriated them.

(33) So Laban went into Jacob's tent and Leah's tent and the tents of the two maidservants; but he did not find them. Leaving Leah's tent, he entered Rachel's tent. (34) Rachel, meanwhile, had taken the idols and placed them in the camel cushion and sat on them; and Laban rummaged through the tent without finding them. (35) For she said to her father, "Let not my lord take it amiss that I cannot rise before you, for the period of women is upon me." Thus he searched, but could not find the household gods.

(Gen. **31**: 3–35)

35 God said to Jacob, "Go up promptly to Bethel and remain there; and build an altar there to the God who appeared to you when you were fleeing from your brother Esau." (2) So Jacob said to his household and to all who were with him, "Rid yourselves of the alien gods in your midst, purify yourselves, and change your garments. (3) Let us promptly go up to Bethel, and I will build an altar there to the God who answered me when I was in distress and who has been with me wherever I have gone." (4) They gave to Jacob all the alien gods that they had, and the rings that were in their ears, and Jacob buried them under the terebinth that was near Shechem. (5) As they set out, a terror from

God fell on the cities round about, so that they did not pursue the sons of Jacob.

(6) Thus Jacob came to Luz — that is, Bethel — in the land of Canaan, he and all the people who were with him. (7) There he built an altar and named the site El-bethel, for it was there that God had revealed to him when he was fleeing from his brother.

(8) Deborah, Rebekah's nurse, died, and was buried under the oak below Bethel; so it was named Allon-bacuth.

(Gen. 35: 1–8)

(14) And Jacob set up a pillar at the site where He had spoken to him, a pillar of stone, and he offered a libation on it and poured oil upon it. (15) And Jacob gave the site, where God had spoken to him, the name of Bethel.

(16) They set out from Bethel; but when they were still some distance short of Ephrath, Rachel was in childbirth, and she had hard labor. (17) When her labor was at its hardest, the midwife said to her, "Have no fear, for it is another boy for you." (18) As she was breathing her last — for she was dying — she named him Ben-oni; but his father called him Benjamin. (19) Thus Rachel died. She was buried on the road to Ephrath — now Bethlehem. (20) Over her grave Jacob set up a pillar; it is the pillar at Rachel's grave to this day.

(Gen. 35: 14–20)

(27) And Jacob came to his father Isaac at Mamre, at Kiriath-arba — now Hebron — where Abraham and Isaac had sojourned. (28) Isaac was a hundred and eighty years old (29) when he breathed his last and died. He was gathered to his kin in ripe old age; and he was buried by his sons Esau and Jacob.

(Gen. 35: 27–29)

Appendix B.
TRADITIONAL GENEALOGICAL
TABLE OF THE PATRIARCHS

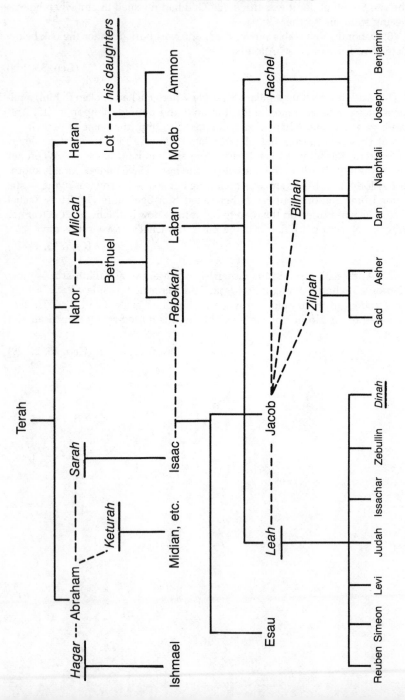

GLOSSARY

SUMERIAN TERMS

lukur	title of woman in religious order
lugal	great man; warrior, leader, king
dingir	(human) deity
gipar	storehouse, sanctuary group of trees (grove)
guenna	throne room
gagia	cloister
gigunu	great reed house; (shrine) sacred nuptial chamber of deities
é-gipar	shrine-house sanctuary on earth corresponding to *gigunu*
en	(feminine or masculine) title of religious persons who, highest in rank of clergy, officiated as deity or spouse of deity
mē	the functions of office/divine attributes

AKKADIAN TERMS

Many of the words in this list were borrowed from Sumerian and Akkadianized, just as English has borrowed and adapted many words.

enu (masculine)	human spouse of deity
entu (feminine)	human spouse of deity
naditu	title of woman in religious order

SARAH THE PRIESTESS

ugbabtu	title of woman in religious order
giparu	storehouse, shrine of Goddess on earth
šarratu	queen
terḫatu	bride-price, dowry
zittu	inheritance
šugetu	lay priestess
ziqqurat	ziggurat; stepped pyramid
gagu	cloister
giguna	great reed house, shrine
šarrat-é-ki-ùr	queen of the reed hut or house *(é-ki-ùr)*

HEBREW WORDS

kohenet	priestess *(kahina* in Arabic)
kohen	priest
bereshith	coming into being, beginning
teraphim	sacred statuary
battim	houses
malkah	queen
shifhah	handmaid
amah	slave
ben-amah	son of a slave
nasi	official, elevated rank
zonah	prostitute
qedeshah	holy woman; / sacred prostitute
lekh, lekhah	walk, go forth
pqd (paqad)	the verb used for coitus in Judges 15:I (according to Cyrus Gordon), and to be understood similarly in the present context.
mshq (mesaheq)	playing, mocking, impurity, but also used in the sense of sexual fondling in Gen. 26:8.

GODDESSES

Astarte	Canaanite
Ashtoreth	Hebrew Astarte (mentioned 9 times in Bible)

164

Asherah	Canaanite; her essence perceived in trees or posts. Mother of Astarte and Anath. Also goddess of the Sea, or called simply Elath (Goddess). Mentioned (mostly as object or symbol) forty times in the Bible.
Anath	originally a separate goddess from Astarte
Nikkal	Canaanite. Semitic rendition of Ningal. Moon Goddess from kingdom of Ugarit (modern Rash Shamra).
Ashratum	Babylonian Asherah
Bau	Sumerian. Goddess of Lagash.
Duttur	Akkadian. Personified ewe. Mother of Dumuzi.
Atharath	Southern Arabian Asherah
Inanna (or Innin)	Sumerian; daughter of Ningal and Nanna of Ur. Goddess of Kish and Uruk. Many titles including Queen of Heaven. Sister of chthonic goddess Eresh-kigal. Goddess of love and light, of war and strife.
Ishtar	Akkadian. Identified with Inanna by Sargon I. Identified with morning star *(Dilbah)* and evening star *(Zib)*.
Ninsuna	Sumerian. Lady of the Wild Cows. Claimed as mother by Gilgamesh and Shulgi. Goddess of wisdom.

GODS

El Shaddai	God of the mountain or breast. Personal God of Abram; brought Abram out of Mesopotamia and gave him the land of Canaan. Generally rendered "Almighty" in English.
Dumuzi	Sumerian; originally a minor god who later became the spouse of Inanna. A dying and resurrecting god. Meaning of name mostly rendered "the true son." Son of Duttur. God of shepherds, dates.
Nanna	Sumerian; tutelary God of Ur. Moon God. Husband of Moon Goddess Ningal and father of Inanna.

Sin	Akkadian; equivalent of Nanna
Tammuz	Syrian; dying and resurrecting God. Semitic equivalent of Dummuzi.
Amaushumgalanna	Sumerian; closely connected with the date palm and originally distinct from Dumuzi. His name means "mother of the date clusters. "
Yarih	Canaanite (from kingdom of Ugarit). Moon God.
Yahweh	God of Israelites (Jehovah)

NOTES

PART ONE

1. For a survey on methods and techniques in biblical interpretation see David Bakan, Chapter 6, "On Interpretation," in *And They Took Themselves Wives* (San Francisco: Harper & Row, 1979), pp. 51-53, and 64 in particular.

2. Harry M. Orlinsky, *Ancient Israel* (Ithaca, N.Y.: Cornell University Press, 1968), pp. 16, 17, 23.

3. Cyrus H. Gordon, *Ugaritic Literature: A Comprehensive Translation of the Poetic and Prose Texts* (Rome: Pontificium Institutum Biblicum, 1949), p. 7.

4. See Appendix A for complete texts. All translations of biblical passages are from *The Torah: The Five Books of Moses* (Philadelphia: The Jewish Publication Society of America, 1962), unless otherwise specified.

5. E. A. Speiser, *Genesis,* in *The Anchor Bible* (Garden City, New York: Doubleday & Co., 1964), p. xxxii.

6. E. A. Speiser, "The Wife-Sister Motif in the Patriarchal Narratives," in A. Altman (ed.), *Biblical and Other Stories* (Boston: Harvard University Press, 1963), pp. 15-28.

7. Speiser, *Genesis,* p. 92.

8. *Ibid.,* p. 94.

9. *Ibid.,* p. 93, or "The Wife-Sister Motif in the Patriarchal Narratives," p. 28. Speiser's explanation does not apply to this issue. The two rulers reproached the patriarchs for having represented the women as their sisters *and not their wives,* so that the rulers felt free to marry or to incorporate the women into their harems. Enhancement of status by sistership standing has no relevance to the problem presented in these stories.

10. D. Freedman, "A New Approach to the Nuzi Sistership Contract," *The Journal of the Ancient Near Eastern Society of Columbia University* (1970), pp. 80-84.

11. S. Greengus, "Sisterhood Adoption at Nuzi and the 'Wife-Sister' in Genesis," *The Hebrew Union College Annual* (1975).

12. T. J. Meek, *Hebrew Origins* (New York: Harper and Row, First Harper Torchbook, 1960).

167

13. Cyrus H. Gordon, "Abraham and the Merchants of Ura," *Journal of Near Eastern Studies* 17 (1958), pp. 28-31; W. F. Albright, "Hebrew Beginnings," in *The Biblical Period from Abraham to Ezra* (New York: Harper Torchbooks, 1963), pp. 1-9.

14. Albright, *The Biblical Period from Abraham to Ezra*, p. 6.

15. *The Interpreter's Dictionary of the Bible* (Nashville: Abingdon Press, 1962), Vol. 3, pp. 498, 617.

16. Speiser, *Genesis*, p. 80.

17. Since the mothers of the women are not mentioned it is not possible to identify their origins matrilineally. Like Sarah and Abram it is possible that Rebekah and Laban also had different mothers.

18. Gordon, *Ugaritic Literature*, p. 63, n. 1.

19. W. F. Albright, *The Archaeology of Palestine* (Gloucester, Mass.: Peter Smith Publisher, 1971), pp. 104-5.

20. R. Patai, *The Hebrew Goddess* (New York: KTAV Publishing House, 1967), p. 59.

21. Sir C. Leonard Woolley, *The Sumerians* (New York: W. W. Norton, 1965), p. 107, 129.

22. S. N. Kramer, *The Sumerians: Their History, Culture and Character* (Chicago: University of Chicago Press, 1963), p. 140.

23. Speiser, *Genesis*, p. 98, for example.

24. *The Pentateuch and the Haftorahs*, edited by J. H. Hertz (London: Oxford University Press, 1929), p. 141, n. 3; *The Torah*, p. 25, n.a. See also: Speiser, *Genesis*, p. 117, n. 3, where the Hebrew *ibbāne* is translated as "I shall be built up."

25. G. R. Driver and J. C. Miles, *The Babylonian Laws*, Section 191 (London: Oxford University Press, 1955), Vol. 2, p. 75, n.f. Subsequent quotation from the Babylonian Laws are from Driver and Miles' translation and commentary unless otherwise specified. Note that the "Laws" of Hammurapi are simply a codification of some ancient oral traditions and new regulations.

26. Louis Ginzberg, *The Legends of the Jews* (Philadelphia: The Jewish Publication Society of America, 1909), Vol. 1, p. 223.

27. Driver and Miles, *The Babylonian Laws*, p. 57.

28. J. van Seters, "The Problem of Childlessness in Near Eastern Law and the Patriarchs of Israel," *Journal of Biblical Literature* 87 (1968), p. 404.

29. T. L. Thompson, *The Historicity of the Patriarchal Narratives* (Berlin and New York: Walter de Gruyter, 1974), p. 262.

30. R. Patai, *Sex and Family in the Bible and the Middle East* (New York: Doubleday & Co., 1959), p. 127.

31. *The Pentateuch and the Haftorahs*, p. 176; *The Torah*, p. 34.

32. The Biblical reading *mesaheq* is used as a euphemism for sexual activity in Gen. 26:8 in regard to Rebekah and Isaac.

33. K. E. Paige and J. M. Paige, *The Politics of Reproductive Ritual* (Berkeley: University of California Press, 1981), p. 147 ff.

34. Speiser, *Genesis*, 157.

35. F. Rue Steele, "The Code of Lipit-Ishtar," *American Journal of Archaeology*, 52 (1948), p. 3.

36. K. Gough, "Variation in Interpersonal Kinship Relationships," in *Matrilineal Kinship*, edited by D. M. Schneider and K. Gough (Berkeley: University of California Press, 1961). "Only children of slaves' wives seem traditionally to have retained permanent obligations to the father and his lineage," (p. 581). Also the Code of Hammurapi, nos. 170-71, would permit Abram to recognize Ishmael as his son.

37. The birthright, though an accident of nature, was obviously not irrevocable; it could be traded or sold. The blessing, on the other hand, once given was final. Simpson questions the need for the blessing, since Jacob already had the birthright and proposes that Genesis 27:1-40 was a later insertion of J and E, since the tale was morally objectionable. An attempt was consequently made to shift the blame on to Rebekah who, "as a woman, might be expected to have questionable morals and who was of little concern to her descendants." C. Simpson, *Interpreter's Bible*, Vol. 1, Genesis (New York: Abingdon Press, 1951), pp. 668-79. It would seem, however, that the question resides first in the consequences afforded the owner of the birthright and the blessing, *bekora* and *beraka* being two different issues. Rebekah was concerned with the latter, the blessing, and not with the trade of the birthright. It would seem that the blessing held different implications to those of the birthright (primogeniture), the latter being a prerequisite for inheritance of property.

38. K. Gough, "Nayar, Central Kerala," in Schneider and Gough, *Matrilineal Kinship*, p. 365. "Cross-cousin marriage, when it is arranged by the senior generation, suggests an interest in prolonging the ties brought about by paternity and by matrilineal kinship." So Isaac sends Jacob to choose a wife from the house of his mother's brother, Laban.

39. Speiser, *Genesis*, p. 193 (birthright), p. 205 (ruse), p. 214 (Jacob to Laban), p. 211 (exile).

40. J. Gray, *The KRT Text in the Literature of Ras Shamra* (Leiden: E. J. Brill, 1964), Vol. 5, p. 4.

41. *Ibid.*, L. 15, p. 19.

42. Speiser, *Genesis*, pp. 193, 194 n. 22.

43. E. Schusky, *Manual for Kinship Analysis* (New York: Holt, Rinehart & Winston, 1965), p. 79.

44. Lord Raglan, "Kinship and Inheritance," in *Studies in Kinship and Marriage*, edited by I. Schapera, (London: Royal Anthropological Institute of Great Britain and Ireland, 1963), pp. 94-96, for various forms of ultimogeniture.

45. Cf. Deut. 21:16, in which the right of inheritance was given to the firstborn, thus excluding the possible intention of the testor to endow a younger child.

46. Mahalath (Gen. 28:9) and Basemath (Gen. 36:3-4) are both described by the same author, *P*, as being the daughter of Ishmael, sister of Nebaioth,

and wife of Esau. It is not clear whether this is the same woman with two names or two sisters married to the same man.

47. Speiser, *Genesis*, p. 250.
48. A. E. Draffkorn, "Ilani/Elohim," *Journal of Biblical Literature* 76 (1957), pp. 216-24.
49. M. Greenberg, "Another Look at Rachel's Theft of the Teraphim," *Journal of Biblical Literature* 81 (1962), pp. 242-43.
50. Thompson, *The Historicity of the Patriarchal Narratives*, p. 278.
51. *Ibid.*, p. 274.
52. Driver and Miles, *The Babylonian Laws*, cf., "Inheritance of Daughters," pp. 335-41, but especially p. 337.
53. Lord Raglan, *Studies in Kinship and Marriage*, p. 95, states that among the Khasi and Garos tribes of Assam, India, the principal heir is the youngest daughter: "The religious duties fall to the youngest daughter and she is bound to perform the family ceremonies and propitiate the family ancestors."
54. C. Oopong, *Marriage Among the Matrilineal Elite*, Cambridge Studies in Social Anthropology 8 (London: Cambridge University Press, 1974), p. 20. Wives are noted to be well aware of their diminishing rights as kinswomen. See also K. Gough, "The Modern Disintegration of Matrilineal Groups," in Schneider and Gough, *Matrilineal Kinship*, pp. 631-52.
55. D. M. Schneider, "Introduction," in Schneider and Gough, *Matrilineal Kinship*, p. 14.
56. Paragraph 170 of the Hammurapi Code provides that the children of a slave, if accepted by their father, are to share equally with the children of the wife in the father's estate as his heirs. That Ishmael did not inherit, because of a decision made by Sarah, is an indication that the estate she referred to was her own and not her husband's. In patriarchy, the patriarch's wishes would override his wife's. In a non-patriarchal system, a man's estate would belong to his sister's progeny and thus would not be under his wife's jurisdiction.
57. Speiser, *Genesis*, p. 145.
58. The right to name a child is an exercise of authority. Ishmael was named by an angel (Gen. 16:11). God named Isaac (Gen. 17-19). Rebekah and Isaac named their sons (Gen. 25:25-26). Rachel and Leah named all of their children.
59. *The Interpreter's Dictionary of the Bible*, Vol. 3, p. 409, n. 1.
60. Samuel 13:12-13. This speech is similar in content to the words spoken by the brothers of Dinah after she was raped by Shechem (cf. Gen. 34:7).
61. Although both men are the sons of David, only one, Absalom, is quoted as being the brother of Tamar.
62. E. Leach, "The Legitimacy of Solomon," in *Genesis as Myth and Other Essays* (London: Jonathan Cape, 1969), p. 71, n. xiii. Leach focuses on Tamar's loss of virginity as being Amnon's offense.
63. Marvin H. Pope, *Song of Songs*, in *The Anchor Bible*. Wine is used for the enhancement of love, which simulates and stimulates the divine fertility which sustains life (p. 303).

64. Naamah was subsequently transformed into a she-demon. For further information on the demonic Naamah, see R. Patai, *The Hebrew Goddess*, pp. 229 ff.
65. M. Kay Martin and Barbara Voorhies, *Female of the Species* (New York: Columbia University Press, 1975), p. 7.
66. Note that Bethuel is the youngest child of Milcah.
67. *The Interpreter's Bible*, Vol. 1, p. 646. Simpson suggests that Bethuel is a substitution for Laban in Gen. 22:22.
68. In the Song of Songs the bride's mother and brothers are mentioned, but not her father.
69. According to Philo, Bethuel, meaning "daughter of God," was the name given by the oracles to Wisdom (i.e., Sophia) and is a feminine name. Cf. *Philo*, translated by F. H. Colson and G. H. Whitaker (New York: G. P. Putnam's Sons, 1934), vol. 5, para. 50-51-52, p. 37, for a misogynistic argument on the name.
70. Speiser, *Genesis*, p. 184.
71. Chie Nakane, *Garo and Khasi: A Comparative Study in Matrilineal Systems* (Paris: Cahiers de l'Homme, Nouvelle Série V. 1967), p. 125.
72. *Ibid.*, p. 127: "As far as the residence of women is concerned the Khasi keep to strict descent rule; two women belonging to different descent groups never live together." The house of Sarah was not the house of Hagar. Isaac belongs to Sarah's house and therefore takes his wife to his mother's house to continue her lineage.
73. Ginzberg, *The Legends of the Jews*, p. 297.
74. K. Gough, "Preferential Marriage Forms," *Matrilineal Kinship*, pp. 623-24, for discussion concerning sororal polygyny among the Navaho, Bemba, and Truk.
75. Claude Levi-Strauss, *The Elementary Structures of Kinship*, trans. by J. Harle Bell and J. R. von Struner; Rodney Needham (ed.) (Boston: Beacon Press, 1969); cf. Chap. 24 for the implications of the terms "bone" and "flesh."
76. David F. Aberle, "Matrilineal Descent in Cross-Cultural Perspective," in Schneider and Gough, *Matrilineal Kinship*, p. 719. Aberle claims strong and significant relationship between sororal polygyny and matrilocality in his research.
77. Oopong, *Marriage Among the Matrilineal Elite*, p. 42. "Most legal authorities support the view that the inheriting matrilineal segment is composed of the mother of the deceased and all persons male or female descended from her in the female line. It is only in the total absence of such matrikin that a man's children have any right to inherit his personally acquired property; similarly spouses continue to be barred from the rights of inheritance." Following the matrilineal descent system, Jacob would have been barred from the inheritance rights of his wives. Laban would (together with Rebekah) have inherited from his mother. His daughter(s) would inherit from him, or rather, from his wife. The inheritance demanded by Rachel and Leah and the *teraphim* taken by Rachel would have been that which descended through the female line and which belonged to their mother; it should belong to themselves and their children rather than

Laban. According to Oopong, there is massive evidence of discontent in West Africa at the continuation of this matrilineal inheritance system. The same discontent is evidenced in the situation we encounter between Laban and his daughters.

78. W. C. Graham and H. G. May, *Culture and Conscience* (Chicago: University of Chicago Press, 1936), p. 94. The authors suggest that the story of Rachel taking the *teraphim* to Canaan may have some connection with the introduction of a mother-goddess into Palestine.

79. Bakan, *And They Took Themselves Wives*, p. 145.

80. Oopong, *Marriage Among the Matrilineal Elite*, p. 29. "Segments of the most inclusive matrilineage are defined by reference to a recent ancestress, to whom members trace their matrilineal descent." In this case, Rachel would have been the ancestress; Jacob blessed her grandchildren putting the younger before the elder, rather than Leah's whose eldest son would have been blessed according to patrilineal usage.

PART TWO

1. E. O. James, *The Ancient Gods: The History and Diffusion of Religion in the Ancient Near East and the Eastern Mediterranean* (New York: G. P. Putnam's Sons, 1960), p. 92.

2. Albright, *The Biblical Period from Abraham to Ezra*, p. 2; Speiser, *Genesis*, p. xiii; Orlinsky, *Ancient Israel*, p. 16.

3. I. J. Gelb, *A Study of Writing* (Chicago: University of Chicago Press, 1965), pp. 62-63.

4. H. W. F. Saggs, *The Greatness that Was Babylon* (New York: New American Library, Mentor Books, 1962, p. 51.

5. Th. Jacobsen, *The Treasures of Darkness: A History of Mesopotamian Religion* (New Haven: Yale University Press, 1976), p. 77.

6. C. S. Chard, *Man in Prehistory* (New York: McGraw-Hill, 1975, p. 246. Chard is referring to a period in time that preceded the rise of urbanism. Cf. pp. 252-53.

7. H. Frankfort, *The Birth of Civilization in the Near East* (N.Y.: Doubleday & Co., Anchor Books, 1956), pp. 78-80. The evolutionary theory held by Frankfort, Jacobsen, and others is not acceptable to many schools of thought. For my personal view, see note 6.

8. Th. Jacobsen, *Toward the Image of Tammuz and Other Essays on Mesopotamian History and Culture* (Cambridge, Mass.: Harvard University Press, 1970), pp. 141-42. The king at this point is not, however, the absolute ruler (cf. Saggs, *The Greatness that was Babylon*, p. 59).

9. Jacobsen, *The Treasures of Darkness*, p. 6.

10. S. J. Teubal, "Women, The Laws and the Ancient Near East," in *Fields of Offerings: Studies in Honor of Raphael Patai*, (Madison, N.J.: Fairleigh Dickinson University Press, A Herzl Press Publication, 1983), p. 305.

11. W. W. Hallo and J. J. A. van Dijk, *The Exaltation of Inanna* (New Haven: Yale University Press, 1968), p. 1.

12. *Ibid.*, p. 7.
13. *Nin-me-šár-ra*. For translation and transliteration, cf. Hallo and van Dijk, *The Exaltation of Inanna*, chap. 2.
14. J. J. Finkelstein, "Late Old Babylonian Documents and Letters," *Yale Oriental Series, Babylonian Texts*, vol. 13 (New Haven: Yale University Press, 1972), p. 7.
15. R. Harris, "The Organization and Administration of the Cloister in Ancient Babylonia," *Journal of the Economic and Social History of the Orient* 6:2 (1963), p. 122, n. 2.
16. Jacobsen, *Toward the Image of Tammuz*, p. 375, n. 32.
17. Cf. Shin T. Kang, *Sumerian Economic Texts from the Drehem Archive: Sumerian and Akkadian Cuneiform Texts in the Collection of the World Heritage Museum of the University of Illinois*, vol. 1 (Urbana: University of Illinois Press, 1972). In particular, "The Role of Women in the Drehem Texts," p. 261.
18. Jacobsen, *Treasures of Darkness*, pp. 24, 35.
19. S. H. Hooke, *Babylonian and Assyrian Religion* (Norman Okla.: University of Oklahoma Press, 1963), pp. 41-43.
20. M. Jastrow, Jr., *Aspects of Religious Belief and Practice in Babylonia and Assyria* (New York: G. P. Putnam's Sons, Knickerbocker Press, 1911), p. 143.
21. E. Douglas Van Buren, "The Sacred Marriage in Early Times in Mesopotamia," *Orientalia* (Rome: Ponticum Institutum Biblicum, 1944), pp. 52-55.
22. Frankfort, *The Birth of Civilization in the Near East*, p. 297.
23. A Tammuz liturgy enumerates eleven kings of this period (ca. 2100 B.C.) from Ur-Nammu to Pur-Sin of Isin, bearing the divine determinative before their names (cf. Hooke, *Babylonian and Assyrian Religion*, p. 31). The theme of the dying and resurrecting god is not relevant to our analysis of the Genesis narratives unless the sacrifice of Isaac (Gen. 22) can be interpreted as such. This conjecture is difficult to substantiate, since Isaac is the son but not the bridegroom of Sarah.
24. Van Buren, "The Sacred Marriage in Early Times in Mesopotamia," pp. 36-37.
25. *Ibid.*, p. 40.
26. Robert Graves, *The White Goddess* (New York: Farrar, Straus and Giroux, 1966), p. 270.
27. Sir C. Leonard Woolley, *Ur of the Chaldees* (New York: W. W. Norton, Norton Library, 1965), p. 169.
28. W. F. Albright, *Archaeology, Historical Analogy and Early Biblical Tradition* (Baton Rouge: Louisiana State University Press, 1968), p. 35.
29. Graves, *The White Goddess*, p. 180.
30. James, *The Ancient Gods*, p. 242.
31. *Ibid.*, p. 245.
32. *Ibid.*, pp. 249, 252.
33. C. H. Gordon, *The Common Background of Greek and Hebrew Civilizations* (New York: W. W. Norton, 1965), p. 121, states that poetry is a regular

medium for oracles in Hebrew, Greek, and other ancient Near Eastern literatures.

34. Raphael Patai summarizes the attacks of biblical reformers, kings, and prophets on Asherah religion. See *The Hebrew Goddess* (New York: KTAV Publishing House, Inc., 1967), pp. 29-52.

35. James, *The Ancient Gods*, p. 252, believes there is little doubt that mountains, caves, oracle trees, wells, and stones sacred to the Canaanites were taken over by the Israelites. In this category I would include the grove at Mamre and the Machpelah cave.

36. Bakan, *And They Took Themselves Wives*, p. 73.

37. *The Interpreter's Dictionary of the Bible*, Vol. 3, pp. 573-74.

38. W. C. Graham and H. G. May, *Culture and Conscience: An Archaeological Study of the New Religious Past in Ancient Palestine* (Chicago: University of Chicago Press, 1936), p. 94. The authors suggest that the story of Rachel taking the *teraphim* to Canaan may have some connection with the introduction of a goddess into Palestine.

39. Jacobsen, *Treasures of Darkness*, p. 25.

40. *Ibid.*, p. 26. Also, A. Poebel, *Historical Texts* (Philadelphia, 1914), p. 125, suggests "wild cow" is a poetical term for "the strong one."

41. R. Harris, "The Organization and Administration of the Cloister in Ancient Babylonia," *Journal of Economic and Social History of the Orient* 6, Part 2, July 1963, p. 8.

42. *Ibid.*

43. Patai, *The Hebrew Goddess*, p. 295, n. 56.

44. The *gigunu* was an especially sacred chamber within the temple complex (*gipar*) in which the more intimate rites of the sacred marriage were carried out.

45. Woolley, *The Sumerians*, p. 16.

46. It is difficult to conjecture which Goddess was associated with Sarah. The moon Goddess Ningal of Ur and Haran, known as Nikkal in Canaan, is a strong possibility, as I believe will become evident in the following chapters.

47. L. Ginzberg, *The Legends of the Jews* (New York: Simon and Schuster, 1956), p. 142.

48. Jacobsen, *Toward the Image of Tammuz*, p. 322, n. 4.

49. Van Buren, "The Sacred Marriage in Early Times in Mesopotamia," p. 25.

50. Patai, *Sex and Family in the Bible and the Middle East*, pp. 121.

51. Cf. R. Harris, "The Case of Three Marriage Contracts," *Journal of Near Eastern Studies* 33:4 (1974): pp. 363-69.

52. See *The Ancient Near East: An Anthology of Texts and Pictures*, edited by James B. Pritchard (Princeton University Press, 1958), pp. 138-67.

53. J. van Seters, "The Problem of Childlessness in Near Eastern Law and the Patriarchs of Israel," *Journal of Biblical Literature* 87 (1968), p. 403.

54. R. Graves and R. Patai, *Hebrew Myths: The Book of Genesis* (New York: Doubleday & Co., 1964), p. 165.

55. J. H. Hertz, ed., *The Pentateuch and the Haftorahs*, vol. 1 (London: Oxford University Press, 1929), p. 252, n. 3.
56. Mandrakes were used in Ugarit by the priestesses as part of a magic formula and were believed to be endowed with aphrodisiacal properties by the ancient Canaanites. Cf. C. F. A. Schaeffer, *The Cuneiform Texts of Ras Shamra-Ugarit* (London: The British Academy, 1939), pp. 46-48.
57. Harris, "The Organization and Administration of the Cloister in Ancient Babylonia," p. 128.
58. *Ibid.*, p. 121, n. 2.
59. Diane Wolkstein and Samuel Noah Kramer, *Inanna: Queen of Heaven and Earth. Her Stories and Hymns from Sumer* (N.Y.: Harper & Row, 1983), p. 155.
60. Saggs, *The Greatness that Was Babylon*, p. 332.
61. Wolkstein & Kramer, *Inanna*, p. 173.
62. Anton Moortgat, *The Art of Ancient Mesopotamia* (N.Y.: Phaidon Publishers, Inc., 1969), p. 12, and plates 19, 20, 21.
63. *Ibid.*
64. Jacobsen, *The Treasures of Darkness*, p. 24.
65. Jacobsen, *Toward the Image of Tammuz*, p. 29. Amaushumgalanna is also thought to mean, "the true son."
66. Jacobsen, *The Treasures of Darkness*, p. 26.
67. Saggs, *The Greatness that Was Babylon*, p. 49. Neither Saggs nor Jacobsen mention the two women in the sanctuary but Elizabeth Douglas Van Buren (see reference for 69, page 21) tells us that women attendants ministered to the couple during the ceremony, attested on an Akkadian cylinder seal.
68. *Ibid.*, p. 365. The identification of "Dumuzi" with the "lord" does not appear in Early Dynastic times; J. Renger, p. 258. Kramer, *The Sacred Marriage Rite: Aspects of Faith, Myth and Ritual in Ancient Sumer* (Bloomington: Indiana University Press, 1969), p. 58, where the ritual marriage of *Inanna* to the ruler of Erech and the ruler of Aratta is attested (two generations before Dumuzi became her traditional consort).
69. Van Buren, "The Sacred Marriage in Early Times in Mesopotamia" p. 64.
70. M. E. L. Mallowan, *Baghdader Mitteilungen*, Vol. 3 (1964), p. 65, pl. 8 a-c.
71. Inanna is the daughter of the moon deities Nanna and Ningal, "Great Lady." *Ibid.*, pp. 121-25.
72. Jacobsen, *Toward the Image of Tammuz*, p. 376, n. 32.
73. Van Buren, "The Sacred Marriage in Early Times in Mesopotamia," pp. 5-15.
74. *Ibid.*, pp. 16-17.
75. *Ibid.*, p. 20.
76. *Ibid.*, p. 21. Not all scholars agree on the texts that exclusively describe the ceremony of the *hieros gamos*.
77. *Ibid.*, p. 40.

78. S. N. Kramer, "Sumerian Literature, A General Survey," in *The Bible and the Ancient Near East*, edited by G. E. Wright, (N.Y.: Anchor Books, 1965), p. 342, n. 7.

79. *Ibid.*, pp. 328, 330.

80. Cf. S. N. Kramer, "Literature: The Sumerian Belles-Lettres," in *The Sumerians*, (Chicago: University of Chicago Press, 1963). This chapter is an excellent introduction to the various forms of Sumerian literature.

81. I have used the translation of the "Hymn to Inanna" by D. Reisman (which he calls) "Iddin-Dagan's Sacred Marriage Hymn," *Journal of Cuneiform Studies* 25:4 (1973), pp. 186-92.

82. The poem speaks of the Goddess Inanna only, and not the priestess who presumably represented her. This implies that the priestess who played the role of the Goddess was her incarnation rather than her substitute. It is unlikely that a statue of the Goddess was used in the ceremony since the king had intercourse with Inanna. The king, on the other hand, represented the deified ruler Dumuzi and is visualized as a deified king since he is referred to as Amaushumgalanna and (his human name) Iddin-Dagan.

83. The *me* are interpreted as being holy functions, gifts of civilization, the holy form of things, etc. Diane Wolkstein and Samuel Noah Kramer in *Inanna*, pp. ix, 123, 171, 173, 176, interpret *me* in a number of ways. See pages 16, 17, 18, for a list of *me* given to the Goddess Inanna.

84. Reisman would interpret this phrase as merely an utterance during love making ("Iddin-Dagan's Sacred Marriage Hymn," p. 198). The joy in the festivities which ensue, however, would lead us to believe that the phrase contains more meaning to it than the Goddess's personal feelings. Cf. lines 210-213.

85. S. N. Kramer, *The Sacred Marriage Rite*, p. 79.

86. Van Buren, "The Sacred Marriage in Early Times in Mesopotamia," p. 37. Despite the early date of this publication, I have found it to be the most comprehensive study on the Sacred Marriage and have relied heavily on it.

87. *Ibid.*, pp. 1, 37.

88. *Ibid.*, p. 41.

89. *Ibid.*, pp. 20-23.

90. *Ibid.*, p. 37. He is referred to as Amaushumgalanna (line 187) the god as he lies down beside her. Previously he was the king or Iddin-Dagan or the god.

91. *Ibid.*, p. 41.

92. *Ibid.*, p. 31.

93. *Ibid.*, p. 8. Cf. Jacobsen, *Toward the Image of Tammuz*, pp. 375-76, n. 32.

94. Gordon, *Ugaritic Literature*, 1949, pp. 1, 63.

95. Yarih is the Canaanite counterpart of the Mesopotamian moon-god Nanna-Sin. Yarih, unlike Sin, had no consort until the advent of Nikkal (Ningal), the Mesopotamian moon-goddess. Cf. Gordon, *The Common Background of Greek and Hebrew Civilization*, p.288.

96. Gordon, *The Common Background of Greek and Hebrew Civilizations*, p. 205 (emphasis mine). Gordon states that one thousand shekels were "beyond the range of normal human ability to pay," p. 215.

97. Jacobsen, *Toward the Image of Tammuz*, p. 375, n. 32. The term *en* can refer to a High Priestess or a High Priest.

98. *Ibid.*, p. 376, n. 32. Cf. article by J. Renger, "Heilige Hochzeit," *Reallexikon*, p. 256, para. 16.

99. G. von Rad, *Genesis: A Commentary* (London: S. C. M. Press, 1972), p. 207 (as to whether Sarah was behind the tent door or the tent door was behind the God).

100. Van Buren, *The Sacred Marriage in Early Times in Mesopotamia*, p. 22.

101. E. Douglas Van Buren, "The Giš-ti and the Giš-ka-an-na," *Orientalia: Commentari Periodici Instituti Biblici*, 13:1/2 (1944), p. 283.

102. Van Buren, *"The Sacred Marriage in Early Times in Mesopotamia,"* p. 14.

103. *Ibid.*, p. 16. Cf. *Iddin-Dagan*: Lines 178-79.

104. *Ibid.*, p. 20. Cf. *Iddin-Dagan*: Line 170. In Mamre the visitor is only now acknowledged by Abram as a deity.

105. Gordon, *The Common Background of Greek and Hebrew Civilizations*, p. 245. The verb *pqd* means to command, to visit, etc.

106. C. J. Gadd, "EN-AN-E-DU," *Iraq*, 13:1 (1951), p. 32.

107. A. Heidel, *The Gilgamesh Epic and Old Testament Parallels* (Chicago: University of Chicago Press, 1965), p. 4. See also Jacobsen, *Toward the Image of Tammuz*, p. 26. The title of the Goddess, Ninsuna, meaning "Lady Wild Cow," p. 159, is similar to the name *Leah*, which also means Wild Cow.

108. Jacobsen, *The Sumerian King List* (Chicago: University of Chicago Press, 1939), pp. 90-91.

109. S. L. Ginzberg, *The Legends of the Jews* (Philadelphia: The Jewish Publication Society of America, 1909), p. 316.

110. J. E. Manchip White, *Ancient Egypt: Its Culture and History* (New York: Dover Publications, 1970), p. 43.

111. J. A. Barnes, "Genetrix: Genitor: Nature: Culture?" in *The Character of Kinship*, edited by J. Goody (London: Cambridge University Press, 1973), p. 71, for a survey of doctrines about the process of reproduction as seen in some cultures in which the supernatural is a participant in conception.

112. Marvin H. Pope, *The Song of Songs*, in The Anchor Bible Series (New York: Doubleday & Co., Inc., 1977), p. 433. It is possible that the Canticle is a wedding song in honor of a bride whose marriage has already been consummated. The Shulamite also receives a thousand pieces of silver (lines 8-11-e) as payment for participation in the Sacred Marriage rites. p. 689. See pp. 120, 121, above.

113. Raphael Patai, *Gates to the Old City: A Book of Jewish Legends*, (New York: Avon Books, 1980), pp. 295-296.

114. Jacobsen, *Treasures of Darkness*, p. 141.

115. Rivkah Harris, "The Organization and Administration of the Cloister in Ancient Babylonia" mentions "the longevity of many *naditus*" p. 128. Sarah may very well have lived to a very old age.
116. Ginzberg, *The Legends of the Jews*, p. 136.
117. Van Buren, *The Sacred Marriage in Ancient Mesopotamia*, p. 26. Van Buren explains that the é-ki-ùr, the temple of Ninlil, was the equivalent of the *gu'enna*. The Goddess Ninlil was given the title Queen of *é-ki-ùr*, the mystic chamber in which her marriage to Enlil took place. Sarah is not here being identified with the Mesopotamian Goddess or her shrine. I am simply underlining the possibility that the name Sarah was derived from a title similar to that of a Goddess she may have represented.

PART THREE

1. Carol Ochs, *Behind the Sex of God: Toward a New Consciousness Transcending Matriarchy and Patriarchy* (Boston: Beacon Press, 1977), p. 34.
2. D. N. Freedman, "Ebla is a Four Letter Word," *L S A* (University of Michigan alumni publication, 1977), suggests that the Abraham of Genesis 14 could belong to the third millennium B.C.E. (p. 18). See argument on this point in Chaim Bermant and Michael Weitzman, *Ebla, A Revelation in Archaeology* (New York: Times Books, 1979), pp. 188-189.
3. It is significant to the argument that Isaac was not circumcised in infancy, that the great feast given by Abram celebrated the *weaning* of Isaac rather than his circumcision.
4. J. H. Otwell, *And Sarah Laughed: The Status of Women in the Old Testament* (Philadelphia: Westminster Press, 1977), p. 155.

BIBLIOGRAPHY

ALBRECHT, GEOTZE. "The Laws of Eshnunna," *Annual of American Schools of Oriental Research* (AASOR), 1956.

ALBRIGHT, W. F. *The Biblical Period from Abraham to Ezra.* New York: Harper and Row (Harper Torchbooks), 1963.

_____. *Archaeology, Historical Analogy and Early Biblical Tradition.* Baton Rouge: Louisiana State University Press, 1968.

_____. *The Archaeology of Palestine.* Gloucester, MA: Peter Smith, Publisher, 1971.

_____. "Abraham the Hebrew: A New Archaeological Interpretation," *Bulletin of the American Schools of Oriental Research* 163 (1961).

BAKAN, DAVID. *And They Took Themselves Wives.* San Francisco: Harper and Row, 1979.

BERMANT, CHAIM, and MICHAEL WEITZMAN. *Ebla: A Revelation in Archaeology.* New York: New York Times Book Co., 1979.

BURROWS, M. *The Basis of Israelite Marriage.* New Haven, Conn.: American Oriental Series, 1939.

CASSUTO, U. *The Goddess Anath.* Trans. by Israel Abrahams. Jerusalem: The Magnes Press, The Hebrew University, 1971.

CHARD, CHESTER S. *Man in Prehistory.* New York: McGraw-Hill, 1975.

COLSON, F. H., and G. W. WHITAKER (trans.). *Philo.* Loeb Classical Library, New York: G. P. Putnam's Sons, 1934.

DIAKONOFF, IGOR M. "On the Structure of Old Babylonian Society," in *Ancient Mesopotamia.* Moscow: Nauka Publishing House, 1969.

DINER, HELEN. *Mothers and Amazons: The First Feminine History of Culture.* Trans. by J. P. Lundin. Garden City: A Doubleday Anchor Book, 1973.

DRAFFKORN, ANN E. "Ilani/Elohim." *Journal of Biblical Literature* 176 (1957).

DRIVER, G. R., and J. C. MILES. *The Babylonian Laws: The Translation and Commentary*, Vols. 1 and 2. London: Oxford University Press, 1955.

ELIADE, MIRCEA. *Rites and Symbols of Initiation: The Mysteries of Birth and Rebirth*. New York: Harper and Row, 1958.

ENGELSMAN, JOAN CHAMBERLAIN. *The Feminine Dimension of the Divine*. Philadelphia: Westminster Press, 1979.

FIGULLA, H. H. "Old Babylonian Naditu Records." *Texts from Babylonian Tables in the British Museum*, Part 47. London, 1926.

FINKELSTEIN, J. J. "Late Old Babylonian Documents and Letters," in *Yale Oriental Series: Babylonian Texts*, Vol. 13. (1972) New Haven: Yale University Press.

FRANKFORT, HENRI. *The Birth of Civilization in the Near East*. Garden City N.Y.: Doubleday and Co., 1956.

——— and others. *Before Philosophy*. Baltimore: Penguin Books, 1961.

FRAZER, SIR JAMES GEORGE. *Folklore in the Old Testament*. New York: Macmillan and Co., 1923.

FREEDMAN, DAVID NOEL. "Ebla is a Four Letter Word." *LSA Alumni Publication, The University of Michigan*, 1977.

FREEDMAN, DAVID. "A New Approach to the Nuzi Sistership Contract." *The Journal of the Ancient Near Eastern Society of Columbia University*, 1970.

GADD, C. J. "EN-AN-E-DU." *Iraq* 13:1 (1951).

GELB, I. J. *A Study of Writing*. Chicago: Chicago University Press, 1965.

GINZBERG, LOUIS. *The Legends of the Jews*. Trans. by Henrietta Szold. Vol 1. Philadelphia: The Jewish Publication Society of America, 1909.

GOODY, JACK (ed.). *The Character of Kinship*. Cambridge: Cambridge University Press, 1973.

GORDON, CYRUS H. *The Common Background of Greek and Hebrew Civilizations*. New York: W. W. Norton, 1965.

———. *Ugaritic Literature: A Comprehensive Translation of the Poetic and Prose Texts*. Rome: Pontificum Institutum Biblicum, 1949.

———. "Abraham and the Merchants of Ura." *Journal of Near Eastern Studies* 17 (1958).

GRAHAM, WILLIAM C., and HERBERT G. MAY. *Culture and Conscience: An Archaeological Study of the New Religions Past in Ancient Palestine*. Chicago: Chicago University Press, 1936.

GRAVES, ROBERT. *The White Goddess*. New York: Farrar, Straus and Giroux, 1966.

———, and RAPHAEL PATAI. *Hebrew Myths: The Book of Genesis*. Garden City: Doubleday & Co., 1964.

GRAY, JOHN. *Archaeology and the Old Testament World.* New York: Harper and Row, Harper Torchbooks, 1962.

_____. "The KRT Text in the Literature of Ras Shamra: A Social Myth of Ancient Canaan." *Documents et Monumenta Orientis Antiqui.* Leiden: E. J. Brill, 1964.

GREENBERG, MOSHE. "Another Look at Rachel's Theft of the Teraphim," *Journal of Biblical Literature* 81 (1962).

GREENGUS, SAMUEL. "Sisterhood Adoption of Nuzi and the 'Wife-Sister' in Genesis." *The Hebrew Union College Annual,* 1975.

HALLO, WILLIAM W., and J. J. A. VAN DIJK. *The Exaltation of Inanna.* New Haven: Yale University Press, 1968.

_____. "Biographical Notes on the Naditu Women of Sippar," *Journal of Cuneiform Studies* 15:1 (1962).

HARRIS, RIVKAH. "The Case of Three Marriage Contracts," *Journal of Near Eastern Studies* 33:4 (1974).

_____. "The Organization and Administration of the Cloister in Ancient Babylonia," *Journal of Economic and Social History of the Orient* 6:2 (1963).

_____. "Secularization under Hammurapi," *Journal of Cuneiform Studies* 15:1 (1962).

HAYES, W. C. (ed.). "Papyrus of the Late Middle Kingdom in the Brooklyn Museum," *Papyrus Brooklyn* 35:1446 (1955).

HEIDEL, ALEXANDER. *The Gilgamesh Epic and Old Testament Parallels.* Chicago: University of Chicago Press, 1965.

HERTZ, J. H. (ed.). *The Pentateuch and the Haftorahs.* Vol 1. London: Oxford University Press, 1929.

HOLT, J. M. *The Patriarchs of Israel.* Nashville: Vanderbilt University Press, 1964.

HOOKE, S. H. *Babylonian and Assyrian Religion.* Norman: University of Oklahoma Press, 1963.

_____. *Myth, Ritual and Kingship.* Oxford: Clarendon Press, 1958.

_____. *The Origins of Early Semitic Ritual.* London: Oxford University Press, 1938.

JACK, J. W. "Recent Biblical Archaeology." *The Expository Times* 49 (1937–1938).

JACOBSEN, THORKILD. "Ancient Mesopotamian Religion: The Central Concerns," *Proceedings of the American Philosophical Society* 107 (1963).

_____. *Toward the Image of Tammuz and Other Essays on Mesopotamian History and Culture.* Cambridge, Mass: Harvard University Press, 1970.

_____. *The Treasures of Darkness: A History of Mesopotamian Religion.* New Haven: Yale University Press, 1976.

_____. (ed.) *The Sumerian King List*. Chicago: Chicago University Press, 1939.

JAMES, E. O. *The Ancient Gods: The History and Diffusion of Religion in the Ancient Near Eastern Mediterranean*. New York: G. P. Putnam's Sons, 1960.

JASTROW, MORRIS, JR. *Aspects of Religious Belief and Practice in Babylonia and Assyria*. New York: G. P. Putnam's Sons, Knickerbocker Press, 1911.

JOHNSON, M.D. *The Purpose of Biblical Genealogies*. Cambridge: Cambridge University Press, 1969.

KANG, SHIN T. "Sumerian Economic Texts from the Drehem Archive." *Sumerian and Akkadian Cuneiform Texts in the Collection of the World Heritage Museum of the University of Illinois*, Vol. 1. Urbana: University of Illinois Press, 1972.

KAPADIA, K. M. *The Matrilineal Social Organization of the Napas of Assam*. Bombay: G. R. Bhatkal Co., 1950.

AL-KHALESI, YASIN M. *The Court of Palms*. Malibu, California: Udena Publications, 1978.

KRAMER, SAMUEL NOAH. "Poets and Psalmists: Goddesses and Theologians," in *The Legacy of Sumer*. Ed. Denise Schmandt-Basserat. Malibu, California: Udena Publications, 1976.

_____. "Sumerian Literature, A General Survey," in *The Bible and the Ancient Near East*, ed. G. E. Wright. New York: Anchor Books, 1965.

_____. "Shulgi of Ur: A Royal Hymn and a Divine Blessing," *The Seventy-Fifth Anniversary Volume of the Jewish Quarterly Review*, 1967.

_____. "Cuneiform Studies and the History of Literature: The Sumerian Sacred Marriage," *Proceedings of the American Philosophical Society* 107:6 (1963).

_____. *The Sacred Marriage Rite: Aspects of Faith, Myth and Ritual in Ancient Sumer*. Bloomington: Indiana University Press, 1969.

_____. *The Sumerians: Their History, Culture and Character*. Chicago: The University of Chicago Press, 1963.

LABAT, RENE. *Manuel d'Epigraphie Akkedienne*. Paris: Imprimerie Nationale, 1963.

LA FONTAINE, J. "Descent in New Guinea," in *Character of Kinship*, ed. J. Goody. Cambridge: Cambridge University Press, 1973.

LANSBERGER, BENNO. *Three Essays on the Sumerians*. Malibu: Udena Publications, 1974.

LEACH, EDWARD. "The Legitimacy of Solomon," in *Genesis as Myth and Other Essays*. London: Jonathan Cape, 1969.

LEVI-STRAUSS, CLAUDE. *The Elementary Structures of Kinship*, trans. J. Harle and J. R. von Struner, ed. Rodney Needham. Boston: Beacon Press, 1969.

MACDONALD, ELIZABETH MARY. *The Position of Women as Reflected in Semitic Codes of Law*. Orientals #1. Toronto: University of Toronto Press, 1931.

MCNEIL, W. H., and J. W. SEDLAR (eds.). *The Ancient Near East*. London: Oxford University Press, 1968.

MALLOWAN, MAX EDGAR LUCIEN. *Baghdader Mitteilungen*, Vol 3. Berlin, 1968.

MARTIN, M. KAY, and BARBARA VOORHIES. *Female of the Species*. New York: Columbia University Press, 1975.

MEEK, THEOPHILUS J. *Hebrew Origins*. New York: Harper and Row, 1960.

MOORTGAT, ANTON. *The Art of Mesopotamia*. New York: Phaidon Publishers, 1963.

NAKANE, CHIE. *Garo and Khasi: A Comparative Study in Matrilineal Systems*. Nouvelle Série 5. Paris: Cahiers de l'Homme, 1967.

OCHS, CAROL. *Behind the Sex of God: Toward a New Consciousness Transcending Matriarchy and Patriarchy*. Boston: Beacon Press, 1977.

OCHSHORN, JUDITH. *The Female Experiences and the Nature of the Divine*. Bloomington: Indiana University Press, 1981.

OOPONG, CHRISTINE. *Marriage Among the Matrilineal Elite*. Cambridge Studies in Social Anthropology No. 8. Cambridge: Cambridge University Press, 1974.

ORLINSKY, HARRY M. *Ancient Israel*, second ed. Ithaca, N.Y.: Cornell University Press, 1968.

OTWELL, J. H. *And Sarah Laughed: The Status of Women in the Old Testament*. Philadelphia: Westminster Press, 1977.

PAIGE, KAREN E., and JEFFERY M. PAIGE. *The Politics of Reproductive Ritual*. Berkeley: University of California Press, 1981.

PATAI, RAPHAEL. *Gates to the Old City: A Book of Jewish Legends*. New York: Avon Books, 1980.

———. *The Hebrew Goddess*. New York: KTAV Publishing House, 1967.

———. *Sex and Family in the Bible and the Middle East*. Garden City, N.Y.: Doubleday & Co., 1959.

PLUTARCH. *Lives*. English translation by Bernadette Perrin. New York: Putnam's Sons, 1914–1928.

POEBEL, ARNO. *Historical Texts*. Philadelphia: University Museum, Publications of the Babylonian Section, Vol. 5 (1914).

POPE, MARVIN H. *Song of Songs*. The Anchor Bible. Garden City, N. Y.: Doubleday & Co., 1982.

PRITCHARD, JAMES B. (ed.). *The Ancient Near East: An Anthology of Texts and Pictures*. Princeton, N. J.: Princeton University Press, 1958.

VON RAD, GERHARD. *Genesis: A Commentary*. Trans. John H. Marks. Philadelphia: Westminster Press, 1972.

RAGLAN, LORD. "Kinship and Inheritance," in *Studies in Kinship and Marriage*, ed. I. Schapera. London: Royal Anthropological Institute of Great Britain and Ireland, 1963.

REED, W. *The Asherah of the Old Testament*. Fort Worth, Texas: Christian University Press, 1949.

REISMAN, DANIEL. "Iddin-Dagan's Sacred Marriage Hymn," *Journal of Cuneiform Studies* 25:4 (1973).

RENGER, J. "Heilige Hochzeit." In *Reallexicon der Assyriologie and Vorderasiatischen Archaologie*. Berlin and New York: Walter de Gruyter, 1972-1975.

RICH, ADRIENNE. *Of Woman Born: Motherhood as Experience and Institution*. New York: Bantam Books, 1969.

ROBERTS, J. M. *The Earliest Semitic Pantheon: A Study of Semitic Deities Attested in Mesopotamia Before Ur III*. Baltimore: The Johns Hopkins University Press, 1972.

ROHRLICH-LEAVITT, RUBY. "Women in Transition: Crete and Sumer," in *Becoming Visible: Women in European History*, ed. Renate Bridenthal and Claudia Koonz. Boston: Houghton Mifflin Co., 1977.

ROSALDO, MICHELLE ZIMBALIST, and LOUISE LAMPHERE (eds.). *Women Culture and Society*. Stanford: Stanford University Press, 1974.

SACKS, KAREN. *Sisters and Wives*. Urbana: University of Illinois Press, 1982.

SAGGS, H. W. F. *The Greatness That Was Babylon: A Sketch of the Ancient Civilization of the Tigris-Euphrates Valley*. New York: New American Library, 1962.

SANDARS, N. K. *The Epic of Gilgamesh*. (Introduction and English Translation.) Middlesex, England: Penguin Books, 1972.

SARNA, NAHUM. *Understanding Genesis: The Heritage of Biblical Israel*. New York: Schocken Books, 1970.

SCHAEFFER, CAUDE F. A. *The Cuneiform Texts of Ras-Shamra-Ugarit*. London: The British Academy, 1939.

SCHNEIDER, DAVID M., and KATHLEEN GOUGH (eds.). *Matrilineal Kinship*. Berkeley and Los Angeles: University of California Press, 1961.

SCHUSKY, ERNEST. *Manual for Kinship Analysis*. New York: Holt, Reinhart and Winston, 1965.

SEIBERT, ILSE. *Women in the Ancient Near East*. Leipzig: Edition Leipzig, 1974.

VAN SETERS, JAN. "The Problem of Childlessness in Near Eastern Law and the Patriarchs of Israel," *Journal of Biblical Literature* 87 (1968).

SHANKS, HERSHEL. "The Patriarchs's Wives as Sisters: Is the Anchor Bible Wrong?" *The Biblical Archaeology Review*, 1975.

SIMPSON, C. "Genesis," in *The Interpreter's Bible*, Vol. 1. New York: Abingdon-Cokesbury Press, 1951.

SJOBERG, A. W. and E. BERGMANN, "Collection of the Sumerian Temple Hymns," *Texts from Cuneiform Sources* 8:110. New York: J. J. Augustin Publisher, 1971.

SMITH, S. "The Practice of Kinship in Early Semitic Kingdoms," in *Myth, Ritual and Kinship*, ed. S. H. Hooke. Oxford: Clarendon Press, 1958–1960.

SPEISER, EPHRAIM A. "The Wife–Sister Motif in the Patriarchal Narratives," in *Biblical and Other Studies*, ed. A. Altman. Cambridge Ma: Harvard University Press, 1963.

———. *Genesis: Introduction, Translation and Notes. The Anchor Bible.* New York: Doubleday & Co., 1964.

STEELE, FRANCIS RUE. "The Code of Lipit-Ishtar," *American Journal of Archaeology* 52 (1948).

STONE, MERLIN. *When God Was a Woman.* New York: Dial Press, 1976.

SWINDLER, LEONARD. *Biblical Affirmations of Woman.* Philadelphia: The Westminster Press, 1979.

TEUBAL, SAVINA J. "Women, the Law, and the Ancient Near East," in *Fields of Offering: Studies in Honor of Raphael Patai*, ed. Victor D. Sanua. London and Toronto: Associated University Press, A Herzl Press Publication, 1983.

The Interpreter's Bible. New York: Abingdon-Cokesbury Press, 1951.

The Interpreter's Dictionary of the Bible. Nashville, Tenn.: Abingdon Press, 1962.

The Torah: The Five Books of Moses. Philadelphia: The Jewish Publication Society of America, 1962.

THOMPSON, THOMAS L. *The Historicity of the Patriarchal Narratives: A Quest for the Historical Abraham.* Berlin and New York: Walter de Gruyter, 1974.

VAN BUREN, ELIZABETH DOUGLAS. "The Sacred Marriage in Early Times in Mesopotamia," *Orientalia* 13:4 (1944). Rome: Pontificium Institutum Biblicum.

———. "The giš-ti and the giš-ka-an-na," *Orientalia* 13:1/2 (1944). Rome: Pontificium Institutum Biblicum.

WHISTON, WILLIAM (trans.). *The Works of Flavius Josephus.* New York: International Book Company (undated).

WHITE, J. E. M. *Ancient Egypt: Its Culture and History.* New York: Dover Publications, 1970.

WHITING, R.M. "Tiš-Atal of Nineveh and Babati, Uncle of Šu-sin," *Journal of Cuneiform Studies* 28:3 (1976).

WOLKSTEIN, DIANE, and SAMUEL NOAH KRAMER. *Inanna, Queen of Heaven and Earth: Her Stories and Hymns from Sumer.* New York: Harper and Row, 1983.

WOOLLEY, SIR C. LEONARD. *The Sumerians.* New York: W. W. Norton, 1965.

––––––. *Ur of the Chaldees.* New York: W. W. Norton, 1965.

INDEX

Ishmael, ii, 4, 16, 29, 30, 31, 38, 39, 55, 66, 136
  banishment of, 5, 30, 37, 40–41, 137–138
  circumcision of, 38, 66
Ishtar, 24, 78, 82
Isis, 8
J (redactor), 12, 29, 42, 59, 60, 61, 75
Jacob, i, 6, 15, 59, 60, 61, 63, 64, 67, 68, 84, 139
  burial of, 94
  and Esau, 41–46, 138
  and Esau's birthright, 42, 43, 45
  flight of, from Laban, 46, 50, 64, 67
  grave of, 15
  Isaac's blessing of, 41–46
  marriage of, 42, 45, 46, 64, 66, 137
Jacobsen, Thorkild, 83, 84, 123, 131
  and interpretation of Alabaster vase, 84, 113
James, E. O., 90
Jemdet Nasr period, 73–75, 135
Jerusalem, 30
Jidlaph, 61
Jordan, 28
Josiah, 100
Judah, 60

Kabbalah, 128
Keturah, 41, 94, 95
King David. *See* David
Kiriath-Arba, 25, 28, 97, 132. *See also* Hebron
Kiriath-Sepher, 25, 99
Kish, 24, 78
Kramer, Samuel Noah, 115, 118
Kullab, 128

Laban, 21, 42, 46, 61, 62, 63, 64, 67
  daughters of, 42, 46, 67 (*see also* Leah; Rachel)
  question concerning the heir of, 50–52
  teraphim of, 4, 46, 50–52, 64, 67, 98, 99, 137, 138
Leah, i, 4, 6, 21, 43, 46, 60, 61, 63, 64, 66, 67, 98, 137
  birthplace of, 97
  burial of, 94

CHRONOLOGY

SOUTHERN MESOPOTAMIA

3500 B.C.E. Uruk Period (earliest known writing)
            Early Protoliterate (Uruk IV)

3000   Late Protoliterate (Uruk III–II or Jemdet-Nasr)

SUMER
2900   Early Dynastic I
            Early Dynastic II (general fortification of cities; Gilga-
            mesh)

2400   Early Dynastic III (Ur I Dynasty, theocratic govern-
            ment)

AGADE (AKKAD) DYNASTY
2370   Šarrum-kin (Sargon), 2371–2230

2300
            Naram-Sin, 2291–2255

2290

UR III DYNASTY (SUMER)
2110   Ur-Nammu, 2113–2096

2095   Shulgi, 2095–2048

2029   Ibbi-Sin, 2029–2006

ISIN DYNASTY
1974   Iddin-Dagan, 1974–1954

1934   Lipit-Ishtar, 1934–1924

BABYLON FIRST DYNASTY (OLD BABYLONIAN PERIOD)
1812   Sin-Muballit (Father of Hammurapi), 1812–1793

1792   Hammurapi, 1792–1750

1625   Samsu-ditana (last king of First Dynasty of Babylon),
            1625–1595

p. 73 : Rise of city / king from
rise of alphabet ; why was
alphabet exclusive to males ?
because city implies a fortress to be
defended by brute strength , i.e. male
yet cf p.77 women religious function
important (knowledge of writing)
when a male priest take-over? p.83